Lead the team. Hit the number. Tell the story.

THE $100M PUSH

The Four Decisions PE-Backed SaaS CEOs Make to Deliver Growth in 100 Days

VANESSA GOOLSBY

Broad Book Press, Publisher

Interior layout by Andrew Welyczko, AbandonedWest Creative, Inc.

Paperback ISBN: 9781963549300
eBook ISBN: 9781963549317

Published and printed in the United States.
Library of Congress Control Number: 2025923077

CONTENTS

FIGURE 1: The Push Order of Operations

The Push Order of Operations™

It's the decisions, *not the activities*, that deliver results.

	1 ICP	2 SLA	3 CONTRIBUTION	4 OKRs
DECISION	Ideal Customer Profile	Pipeline Conversion Process	Bookings Contribution Model	Company Priorities to Exit
	Target High-Value Buyers	*Build a Predictable Sales Engine*	*Commit to an Efficient Bookings Plan*	*Plan the CEO's Path to Exit*
EXECUTION	1. Segmentation Analysis 2. ICP Definition 3. Account Scoring 4. Personas & Positioning	5. Lead Response Time 6. Lead Scoring 7. Lead Qualification Training 8. Attribution Reporting 9. Email Rules	10. Bottom-Up Targets 11. Territories & Quotas 12. Marketing Campaign Plan 13. Sales Enablement	14. Company Objectives 15. OKR Project Plan 16. OKR Summary 17. Growth Narrative
MEASUREMENT	› Company Benchmarks › Market Penetration	› Attribution Reporting › SLA Governance	› Contribution Governance › Commercial Board Report	› OKR Governance › Exit Readiness Dashboard
	LEADS IMPROVE	PIPELINE IMPROVES	BOOKINGS IMPROVE	ENTERPRISE VALUE IMPROVES

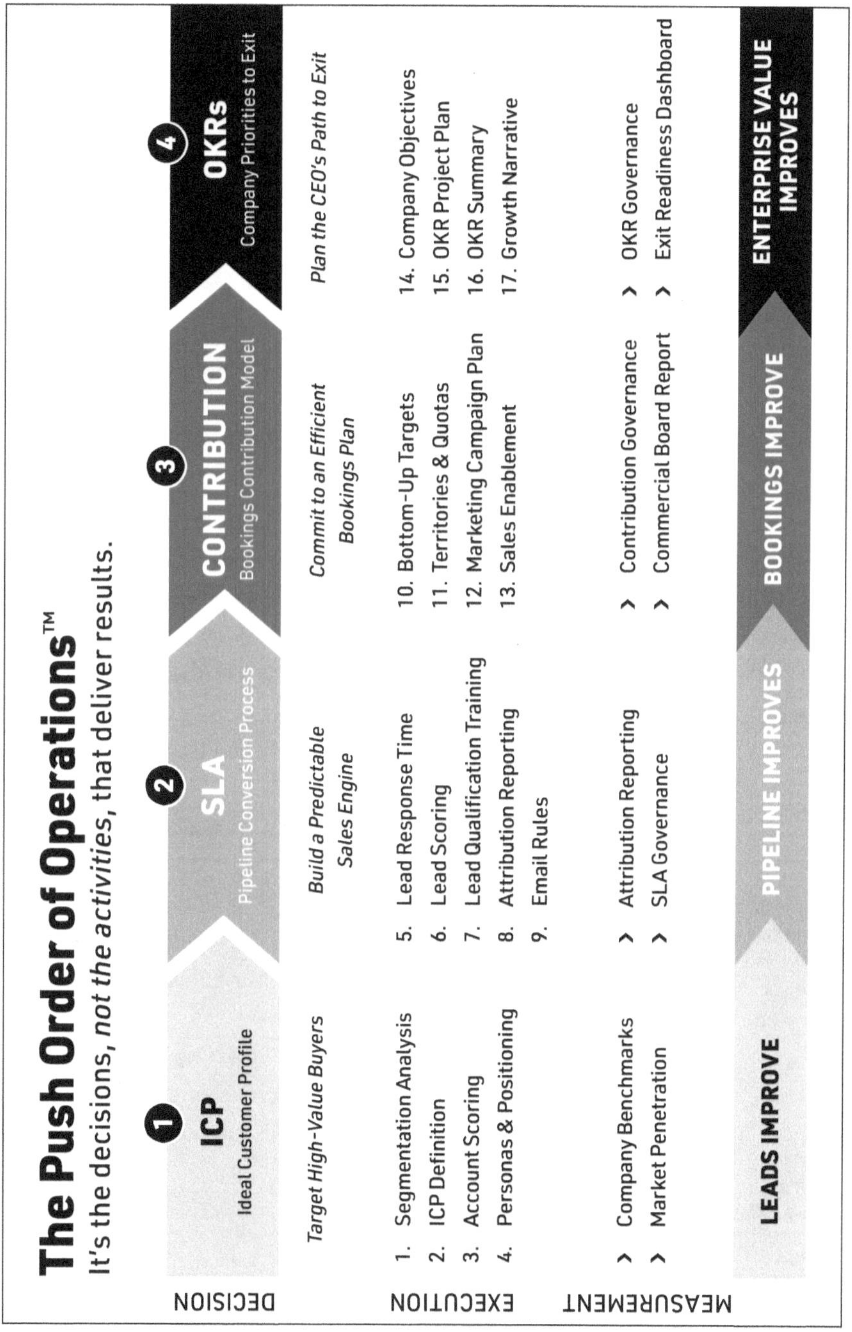

FIGURE 2: The Push 100-Day Plan

Outcome	Growth Decision	Step	Key Milestones	Owner	Duration	Page Number
Target High-Value Buyers	ICP	1	**ICP Workshop**	CEO	1 Day (Day 1)	**46**
		2	Prepare and Append Data	RevOps	7 Days (Days 2–9)	**49**
		3	Segmentation Analysis Complete and ICP Identified	RevOps	40 Days (Days 10–50)	**51**
		4	ICP Board Alignment	CEO	1 Day (Day 51)	**55**
		5	Account Scoring	RevOps	14 Days (Days 52–66)	**60**
		6	Personas & Positioning	Marketing	14 Days (Days 52–66)	**64**
Build a Predictable Sales Engine	SLA	7	**SLA Workshop**	Sales and Marketing	2 Days (Days 67–68)	**105**
		8	Systems Build (CRM and MAP)	RevOps	30 Days (Days 69–99)	**124**
		9	Certified Rep Training	Sales	1 Day (Day 100)	**128**
Create an Efficient Bookings Plan	Contri-bution	10	**Contribution Workshop**	CEO	1 Day (Day 69)	**163**
		11	Territory Planning and Quota Setting	Sales	14 Days (Days 70–84)	**174**
		12	Full-Funnel Campaign Plan	Marketing	30 Days (Days 70–100)	**186**
		13	Contribution Model Tracking	CFO	5 Days (Days 85–90)	**193**
Plan the CEO's Path to Exit	OKR	14	OKR Board Alignment	CEO	1 Day (Day 70)	**222**
		15	**OKR Workshop**	CEO	1 Day (Day 71)	**224**
		16	OKR Tracking	CEO	1 Day (Day 72)	**230**

INTRODUCTION

THE BOARD MEETING took place a year into the hold period of a $35M vertical SaaS business. The founder-CEO was clearly excited about launching a new freemium version of their B2C platform, believing the momentum from a launch like this would raise their profile in the market. For two quarters, they had been pushing their team hard to get it built. Now that it was finally launched, the CEO was looking forward to sharing with the board how well it had been received. They put together board slides packed with praise from users. Quotes praised the new premium features and that those premium features were now available for free. The CEO framed the freemium launch as a brand play: great for reputation and great for delivering more top-of-the-funnel users. Those users and that reputation, they believed, would open the door to more enterprise deals.

The board investors responded to the update with silence. They hadn't backed this company to grow the user base; they backed this company because they believed in the potential to scale its B2B enterprise sales. The deal thesis they sold to their investment committee projected improvements in margin and recurring revenue, both tied directly to the expansion of the

B2B model. And now here they were, four board meetings into their new investment, listening as the CEO excitedly described how the company was moving further away from commitments they had made as investors. They didn't want to talk about user reviews; they wanted to see a clear B2B go-to-market (GTM) plan. Better still, they wanted to see progress against that plan.

Aside from hiring a well-regarded sales leader, the CEO had largely stayed out of the details on B2B. They admitted that B2B wasn't their area of expertise and trusted that the new sales leader was better equipped to scale that side of the business. But the numbers coming in were soft: year-over-year declines, a stagnant pipeline, and missed targets. Perhaps most crucially for the CEO in this particular meeting, there also was no clear narrative about what was going wrong or how they were going to fix it.

Each time the CEO talked about B2C issues like traffic, signups, and social media pick up, the board would bring the conversation back to B2B, asking about enterprise deals, pipeline, and enablement. This went on for the duration, and the meeting was wrapped without incident. There was no argument, no conversation about the value creation plan, nothing to signal that something was amiss. To the CEO, without overt pushback from the board on the B2C launch, the meeting may have even signaled a win. It may have felt like they had successfully made the case for the freemium play.

But after the meeting, once the investors were alone, it only took them a few minutes to agree that the sales leader had to go and to question whether the CEO was capable of building the B2B business the firm had underwritten in the investment.

No one said it to the CEO that day, but this was the meeting that started the clock on their departure.

What I observed in that meeting was an unspoken tug-of-war that I've since seen play out many times: a CEO with a vision moving in a direction that's misaligned with the investment thesis, and their board watching with concern as the gap widens between effort and expected results. The CEO wasn't a bad leader, but they made mistakes common to early growth-stage, PE-backed CEOs scaling to their first $100M:

- They prioritized activity that didn't align with the investment thesis.
- They delegated a strategic area of the business without staying close to execution.
- They failed to create a shared narrative with the board around what was working, what wasn't, and why.

These gaps are common to CEOs navigating this journey to $100M for the first time. They are avoidable with the right framework, with the right decisions, and with a more active leadership stance.

That's what this book is here to provide.

WHY THIS BOOK?

A 2018 survey by AlixPartners revealed that the primary driver of unplanned CEO turnover in private equity portfolio companies was a CEO's inability to execute the new strategy defined by the private equity firm for the business. The book serves as your blueprint for navigating this complexity, ensuring every decision you make drives scalable growth and creates value for your investors, your teams, and your customers.

Scaling from $10M to $100M is one of the most challenging and rewarding journeys a CEO can undertake, particularly in a private equity-backed environment. This book lays out the order of operations for profitable growth, breaking it into clear, achievable steps. It equips you with the tools to lead your team, align your board, and build a company that scales.

As the CEO, you sit at the intersection of strategy, execution, and investor alignment. When you accept a new round of investment, you are no longer just running a company; you're leading a transformation. This book leverages an insider's view of the private equity world combined with the pattern recognition that comes from hands-on experience scaling over 100 portfolio companies to help you anticipate the unspoken investor expectations, avoid common pitfalls, and meet growth objectives with clarity and confidence.

WHAT TO EXPECT IN THIS BOOK

Investors are backing you, as CEO, just as much as they are backing the business you run. This book is a practical guide for CEOs scaling to $100M in a private equity-backed environment. It breaks down what investors expect, what leadership teams need, and what actions you must take to drive new revenue growth and show well to investors. Here's how it's structured.

- **Step-by-Step Guidance:** You'll learn how to lead your team through the Push Order of Operations to scale new bookings in the first 100 days post-investment and to set the foundation for a three- to five-year path to exit.
- **The Four CEO Growth Decisions:** There are four parts in this book. Each part covers a critical decision CEOs must make to prepare the business to scale predictable growth: ICP focus, SLA alignment, Contribution Modeling, and company-wide OKRs.
- **Clear Roles and Actions:** You'll see how to direct your team as CEO, when to engage personally, and what "good" looks like in key functions to know whether it's working.
- **Tools to Build Investor Confidence:** From dashboards to strategic narratives, you'll understand the frameworks and visuals needed to communicate effectively with your board.
- **Real-World Examples:** Case studies and red flag warning signs based on the experience that comes from working with more than 100 software companies to help you avoid common traps.
- **AI Call-Outs:** You'll learn when and how best to insert AI into your standard practices based on what has worked with other companies.
- **Glossary of Terms:** You'll learn the common terms so you can speak the same language as your investor.

Whether you're a founder, a first-time CEO, or a seasoned operator stepping into a PE-backed environment, this book gives you the structure, language, and insight to lead with confidence and deliver results to your board.

HOW TO USE THIS BOOK

This book is not meant to be read cover-to-cover in a single sitting. Instead, it's a practical guide to revisit as you make key decisions during your tenure.

- **For Founders or First-Time CEOs:** Start at the beginning to understand the 100-Day Plan process that starts post-investment.
- **For Experienced CEOs:** Use specific chapters to address current challenges or refine existing strategies.

This is a step-by-step guide for CEOs who are expected to grow new revenue quickly and sustain or scale that growth over a hold period. It helps you focus on the strategic decisions that matter most, direct your team through execution without getting lost in the weeds, and assess whether that execution is on track. You'll also learn how to communicate progress, even through the inevitable slowdowns, in a way that builds board confidence and keeps investors in your corner.

This book follows the structure of a 100-Day Plan, often used at the start of a PE investment when capital is deployed rapidly to close the execution gaps identified in diligence. While this framework is most often used in the first 100 days, though, it's not limited to them. You can apply it any time a lift in pipeline or bookings is needed to regain momentum or scale faster. The 100-Day Plan structure is equally effective in GTM turnarounds, where clarity, speed, and alignment matter most.

As CEO, your role isn't to personally execute the plays outlined in the chapters that follow, but to understand what they require so you can lead decisively, direct your team with confidence, and maintain clear accountability and narrative with your board.

BOOK STRUCTURE

There are four parts to this book, each aligned to one of the four key growth decisions required to scale top-line revenue efficiently and sustainably. Each part includes four chapters.

- The **Introductory Chapter** introduces the growth decision, explains your role as CEO in making it, cautions against common mistakes CEOs make, and shares relevant CEO case studies to help you anticipate what lies ahead.
- The remaining three chapters correspond to the **Decision, Execution**, and **Measurement** phases of that decision—the core stages your team must work through to embed that growth decision into the business.

Every decision is made by guiding your team through a "workshop-plus-data" agenda. This approach serves a dual purpose. It helps you derive key inputs from your team (as experts in their fields) and aligns them with the clear direction that comes from building consensus in a workshop. This lays the foundation for better adoption later in the execution phase. Once a decision is made, the team executes that decision by embedding it into its related activities. This further deepens the alignment and coordination between the different teams.

Finally, you will track the right internal metrics, report progress and outcomes to the board and reinforce your momentum toward the Exit Targets.

Taken together, these chapters help you go beyond strategy. They give you the structure to lead your team through each decision with clarity, urgency, and confidence.

Your work begins in Chapter 1, where you'll learn how investors define success and what it means to take ownership of value creation from day one.

1

THE CEO'S ROLE IN VALUE CREATION

How far away are we from our base case?

Is this the CEO to get us there?

Why did they miss last quarter?

—Examples of questions an investor answers to their investment committee

YOUR INVESTOR is more than just a board member. They become your advocate, championing you and your business to their investment committee (IC), the senior firm leadership your investor answers to. At the start of the investment, your investor ties their reputation to yours to get the deal approved by their IC. Although they root for your success, they will pull back support should they lose confidence in your ability to deliver a return for the firm. From day one, your execution isn't just about running the business. It's about leading your team to the next exit.

This book will help you uncover investor expectations and communicate a story of accountability and progress, even in the messy middle of transformation, to equip you and your investor with the clarity needed to keep track of your growth story. As you work to scale your business, the inevitable dips and stalls will happen. In those moments, you'll need to convey control and accountability to your investor, just as they must do to their IC in those same challenging moments.

You are the keeper of this growth narrative. Your role is to build board confidence and enable your investor to tell your growth story, whether to the IC today or to a prospective buyer tomorrow. However, instinct alone isn't enough to build that story. You'll need a clear, structured path that connects strategic intent to execution.

For most investors, that structure comes in the form of a Value Creation Plan (VCP).

The most certain (and de-risked) path to a strong return is to underwrite a bulletproof value-creation plan (VCP) in due diligence and marry it to a separation plan, a talent strategy, and an execution blueprint specifically calibrated to the VCP's unique requirements. Anything else will sap energy and waste time, blunting the rapid, active management needed from the day the deal is inked.[1]

In short, it's important for you to have a blueprint for commercial execution that hooks into your VCP.

If you're scaling a private equity-backed company, the VCP outlines when specific growth levers need to be pulled during the hold period and what impact those will have on enterprise value (the total worth of the business at exit, calculated by combining equity value and debt, minus cash). It sets the potential price a buyer might pay.

"Value," in the context of the VCP, generally refers to enterprise value. See Figure 4 for a representation of this concept.

VALUE CREATION PLANS VARY IN PRACTICE

Despite how central the VCP is in communicating an investor's expectations, no standards for them exist, and they are inconsistently managed among firms.

....

1 Global Private Equity Report 2025

FIGURE 3: Value Creation Plan Excerpt

100-Day Plan | Value Creation Execution

Year 1		Year 2				Year 3
Q3	Q4	Q1	Q2	Q3	Q4	Q1

Value Creation Levers

1. The Push Framework — Scale GTM execution to Accelerate Bookings Growth and Increase Market Expansion
2. Optimize Pricing to Maximize Lifetime Value (LTV)
3. Hire COO — Build Out Account Management Team to Improve Cross-Sell Revenue
4. Inorganic Growth Through M & A Targets to Take Out Competitors and Expand Into Adjacent Markets
5. Deliver AI-Integrated Product Strategy to Become Market Leader

- **Timing varies:** Some take shape during diligence; others are developed post-close as part of a formal kickoff.
- **Formats vary:** Some firms use milestone-based project plans with owners and KPIs; others have a single roadmap slide or a thick deck with research and narrative; some may provide nothing at all.
- **Ownership varies:** Sometimes a VCP is co-owned with the PE firm or Operating Partner; other times, it's entirely the CEO's responsibility.

What is consistent is that a VCP is the deal's execution roadmap. Its purpose is to anchor on the market-level milestones that must be hit to drive enterprise value and justify the exit valuation. The VCP starts day one post-close of the investment and lasts through exit. In Figure 4, you can see what the full scope of deal lifecycle stages look like.

The Push Framework aligns to the market-level growth milestones common in most deals, particularly for companies scaling from $10M to $100M. Whether or not a formal Value Creation Plan exists, you will need

FIGURE 4: Deal Lifecycle Stages

Deal Lifecycle Stage	Description	CEO Role	Investor Objective
❶ Deal Sourcing	Identify attractive sectors and targets, build thesis, and engage prospects.	Typically not involved yet.	Develop thesis and find compelling targets.
❷ Due Diligence and IC Approval	Assess growth, margin, and risk, finalize IC memo and valuation.	May be interviewed.	Validate assumptions in the thesis. Calibrate risk-return.
❸ Deal Close	Negotiate terms, structure debt, finalize agreements, and close.	Informed of close and introduced to board.	Finalize terms, governance, and alignment.
❹ Year 1: VCP Starts With 100-Day Plan	Establish priorities, team, metrics, and governance model.	Set direction, build trust.	Translate thesis into action. Build. confidence in leadership.
❺ Years 2–5: Scale Phase	Drive execution, ops improvement, product, pricing, and M&A.	Drive people, process, tech playbooks for continued growth.	Hit IRR through profitable growth and transformation.
❻ Exit Prep	Refine reporting, position equity story, launch banker process.	Readies team, metrics, and narrative for buyers.	Maximize exit multiple and return profile.
❼ Exit	Execute sale, IPO, or recap; return capital.	May transition, stay, or roll equity.	Deliver return to LPs.

to learn how to own the commercial transformation, communicate investor-aligned progress, and show well to your board, especially during moments of uncertainty or change.

That alignment starts with understanding how your investors measure success. Behind every deal, there's a financial model that defines what "good" looks like and how quickly it must be achieved.

THE INVESTOR'S YARDSTICK

Even if never shared, your investor built a base case model before closing the deal that was anchored on IRR (Internal Rate of Return) or the estimated rate of return on the investment. To hit that IRR, the base case model probably included:

- Exit year ARR and margin targets
- Retention and growth efficiency benchmarks (e.g., GRR, NRR, LTV:CAC) and the Rule of 40 or equivalent (growth rate + margin)
- Valuation levers (e.g., shift revenue mix toward recurring, grow inorganically through M&A, clean up financial reporting) and associated risks

The VCP, whether formal or informal, is meant to map at a high level the initiatives that de-risk the path to the base case numbers. *The Push Framework* supports the value creation plan by focusing you on the foundations required to enable profitable growth regardless of VCP. It cuts through the noise of data overload by anchoring on a focused set of leading indicators that matter most at this stage of growth.

YOUR ROLE AS CEO

As CEO, it's your job to take ownership of value creation, regardless of whether your investor has a standard Value Creation Plan process in place or not.

Regardless of whether or not your investor works with you to co-develop a VCP, there are two critical inputs you need to ask for to understand what's expected of you from this investment: exit targets and value creation levers. These are typically documented in the investment thesis that was used to win internal IC approval for the deal and will be used to guide you post-close on the investor-side. They represent the foundation of what your investor and their investment committee expect from you over the hold period.

1. **Exit Targets** or ***What Your Investor Expects You to Deliver by Exit:*** These are the headline metrics your investor used to model returns, such as ARR, GRR, NRR, EBITDA margin, and in many cases the Rule of 40 or an equivalent. The investor will have built return scenarios with assumptions about where the company

needs to land on these metrics by the time of exit. You need clarity on these metrics. These are the "north star" outcomes your investor expects you to lead your team toward over the hold period.

2. **Value Creation Levers** or ***How Your Investor Expects You to Deliver Those Outcomes:*** Informed by the market research performed during diligence, these are the long-range, high-level growth levers that form your investor's early hypotheses about how value will ultimately be created. Common examples include:
   a. Pricing optimization
   b. Upmarket expansion into larger accounts
   c. Platform differentiation or rebuilds
   d. Go-to-market redesign (e.g., introducing inside sales or channel partners)

Because they are generally tied to market dynamics, these levers tend to hold true over the hold period unless disrupted by an unforeseen shift in market conditions.

These value creation levers are the ways in which your investor expects the business to be attractive to a new buyer at exit. Some CEOs fall into the trap of treating them as suggestions rather than investor expectations. To ignore them completely will put you in a lonely and defensive position.

The third input you'll need to create long-term value is led by you.

3. **100-Day Plan** or ***How You Will Lead Your Team to Execute the Value Creation Levers:*** This is where you come in. While the investor outlines the destination and the high-level growth levers, it's your job to plot the route. A 100-Day Plan is a structure commonly used in the early days of a PE investment to move quickly against high-priority gaps with fresh investment dollars. The 100-Day Plan is where execution begins. It reflects urgency and sets the tone for the rest of the hold period. This book guides you in building and executing a 100-Day Plan meant to achieve a jump in bookings growth.

Owning the Value Creation Plan means translating investor expectations into an actionable operating system. *The Push Framework* gives you that

FIGURE 5: CEO Artifacts That Translate Investment Thesis into Commercial Execution

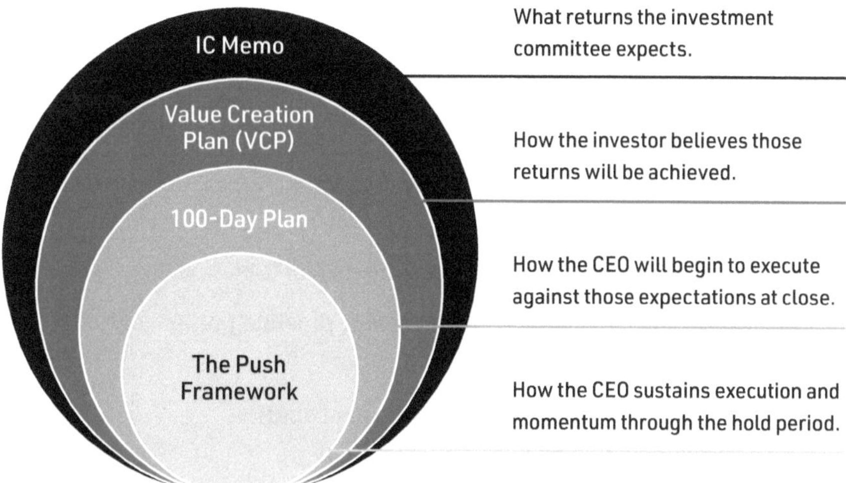

system. It turns abstract levers like "expand upmarket" or "optimize pricing" into a clear sequence of growth decisions that connect your strategy to execution and your execution to investor outcomes.

THE FOUR CEO GROWTH DECISIONS

If you are the CEO of a growth stage SaaS business scaling to $100M, then your investment thesis will inevitably include at least one value creation lever tied to market expansion. That may sound like:

- **Move up-market:** Sell to larger, more complex enterprise accounts.
- **Move down-market:** Simplify a version of the product; oftentimes with a self-serve sales model or inside sales.
- **Expand within your existing market:** Capture more of the same segment.
- **Enter adjacent markets:** Apply the product to new, but related segments.

There are four key growth decisions needed to achieve these expansion levers, which I'm calling the Push Order of Operations. This sequence walks you step-by-step through when to make those decisions, how to direct your team to execute them, and how to measure success of and communicate progress on those decisions to your investor. Figures 6 and 7 gives you a visual look at this system.

Taken in sequence, these decisions help your team:

1. Focus on the highest-value customers *(ICP Decision)*.
2. Align Sales and Marketing to convert pipeline predictably *(SLA Decision)*.
3. Fund the right sources of pipeline contribution *(Contribution Decision)*.
4. Link short-term execution to the long-term exit outcomes *(OKR Decision)*.

When taken in order, these decisions and their subsequent executions also connect your teams in a way that transforms your go-to-market (GTM) processes. When executed, these decisions embed as interlocks between your teams. These connections drive predictable growth over the long-term. Whether you're following the sequence in the first 100 Days post-close or using it to address a slowdown later during the hold period, following this framework in a condensed 100-Day Plan structure moves the company forward quickly and deliberately for the highest and fastest impact.

This system assumes you're in the first 100 days of an investment and therefore walks you through all four decisions. However, each decision within *The Push Framework* can be addressed independently whenever you recognize early signs that your commercial engine is slowing down.

Now that you can see your business from your investor's perspective, you are ready to begin leading your team through the growth decisions that will deliver on their expectations.

FIGURE 6: The Push Order of Operations

The Push Order of Operations™

It's the decisions, *not the activities*, that deliver results.

	1 ICP Ideal Customer Profile	2 SLA Pipeline Conversion Process	3 CONTRIBUTION Bookings Contribution Model	4 OKRs Company Priorities to Exit
DECISION	*Target High-Value Buyers*	*Build a Predictable Sales Engine*	*Commit to an Efficient Bookings Plan*	*Plan the CEO's Path to Exit*
EXECUTION	1. Segmentation Analysis 2. ICP Definition 3. Account Scoring 4. Personas & Positioning	5. Lead Response Time 6. Lead Scoring 7. Lead Qualification Training 8. Attribution Reporting 9. Email Rules	10. Bottom-Up Targets 11. Territories & Quotas 12. Marketing Campaign Plan 13. Sales Enablement	14. Company Objectives 15. OKR Project Plan 16. OKR Summary 17. Growth Narrative
MEASUREMENT	› Company Benchmarks › Market Penetration	› Attribution Reporting › SLA Governance	› Contribution Governance › Commercial Board Report	› OKR Governance › Exit Readiness Dashboard
	LEADS IMPROVE	PIPELINE IMPROVES	BOOKINGS IMPROVE	ENTERPRISE VALUE IMPROVES

FIGURE 7: The Push 100-Day Plan

Outcome	Growth Decision	Step	Key Milestones	Owner	Duration	Page Number
Target High-Value Buyers	ICP	1	**ICP Workshop**	CEO	1 Day (Day 1)	**46**
		2	Prepare and Append Data	RevOps	7 Days (Days 2–9)	**49**
		3	Segmentation Analysis Complete and ICP Identified	RevOps	40 Days (Days 10–50)	**51**
		4	ICP Board Alignment	CEO	1 Day (Day 51)	**55**
		5	Account Scoring	RevOps	14 Days (Days 52–66)	**60**
		6	Personas & Positioning	Marketing	14 Days (Days 52–66)	**64**
Build a Predictable Sales Engine	SLA	7	**SLA Workshop**	Sales and Marketing	2 Days (Days 67–68)	**105**
		8	Systems Build (CRM and MAP)	RevOps	30 Days (Days 69–99)	**124**
		9	Certified Rep Training	Sales	1 Day (Day 100)	**128**
Create an Efficient Bookings Plan	Contri-bution	10	**Contribution Workshop**	CEO	1 Day (Day 69)	**163**
		11	Territory Planning and Quota Setting	Sales	14 Days (Days 70–84)	**174**
		12	Full-Funnel Campaign Plan	Marketing	30 Days (Days 70–100)	**186**
		13	Contribution Model Tracking	CFO	5 Days (Days 85–90)	**193**
Plan the CEO's Path to Exit	OKR	14	OKR Board Alignment	CEO	1 Day (Day 70)	**222**
		15	**OKR Workshop**	CEO	1 Day (Day 71)	**224**
		16	OKR Tracking	CEO	1 Day (Day 72)	**230**

2

THE PUSH

SCALING FROM $10M to $100M ARR is a transformative journey that requires CEOs to adopt an active leadership style.

When you deliberately scale your business to a $100M company, your team will transform as a result. As a private equity-backed CEO, you are seen as the driving force behind this transformation, balancing strategic alignment with investors with hands-on leadership across your teams.

In this chapter, you'll learn what it means to actively push your leadership team, how to "show well" to investors, and how to avoid some of the common mistakes CEOs make when scaling to $100M for the first time.

WHAT IT TAKES TO "SHOW WELL" TO INVESTORS IN THE FIRST 100 DAYS

Few changes are as disruptive to a company as replacing the CEO, yet most CEO turnover in PE-backed firms is unplanned. Six out of 10 CEO replacements occur within the first year, often attributed to poor performance linked to leadership weaknesses such as unfocused execution, lack of urgency, and limited adaptability.[2] If you were CEO during the buy process, your investors probably courted you, built a relationship, and rooted for you. However, their true assessment of your capabilities begins with the first 100 days of investment.

Those first 100 days serve as a proving ground, where you not only lead your team through the four CEO growth decisions but also demonstrate to your investors that you are the leader who can deliver on execution. To "show well" to your investor in this critical period, you must:

- **Act with Urgency**. Push your team to adopt scalable processes and close gaps identified in diligence quickly. Demonstrate control, adaptability, and a bias for action.
- **Demonstrate Operational Excellence.** Lead confidently through the growth decisions. Show control over key metrics, decision-making, and systems execution as you guide the company through strategic maturity.
- **Build Investor Confidence.** Translate the investment thesis into measurable results. Ground your strategy in data, frame challenges as part of the growth story, and clearly communicate how the company will achieve its Value Creation Plan.

Exemplifying these three behaviors to your investors builds their confidence in your ability to scale the business and overcome challenges along the way. To achieve this, you'll need to stay connected with your team and lead them through real transformation. By following the Push Order of Operations, you'll not only build a system for predictable profitable growth, but you'll inadvertently reinforce a culture of transparency, collaboration, and a bias for action within your team. An incredible thing happens for CEOs as they work through this framework and start to see these traits emerge in their leadership team: They find themselves transformed as well.

2 AlixPartners, Leadership and the Future of Value Creation

HOW CEOS SOLVE EXECUTION RISK BY EVOLVING THE TEAM

Throughout the portfolios of various funds, investors and Operating Partners cite execution risk, or lack of urgency and unfocused execution, as the main cause of poor performance.[3] Once the investment closes, investors shift their focus to evaluating how well you and your management team execute.

Scaling a company is about evolving your organization to meet the demands of scale to achieve growth. Growth is the outcome—the evolution of your team is how you get there. For commercial teams, this transformation is guided by the four strategic growth decisions outlined in this book. By leading your team through the Push Order of Operations Framework, you effectively guide and coach your GTM leadership team through the process of maturing the coordination that connects each of their functions.

For companies under $100M, many of the processes referenced in this book may exist in fragments but may lack cross-functional coordination. The transition from working in silos to working in unison is a key marker of maturity. While the following chapters will walk you through the decisions and execution steps that drive alignment, it's important to understand the team values you'll unlock as a result: *Bias for Action, Transparency, and Collaboration.*

Simply by leading the team through the Push Order of Operations, you will embed these values with your leadership team. It's a natural result of the framework. As CEO, you can use your unique position to reinforce these values by approaching the process in a certain way.

HOW CEOS INSTILL THE PUSH TEAM VALUES

- **Bias for Action:** Reduce distractions and maintain focus on your immediate objectives with prioritization. You are the only one with final veto or "de-prioritization" power, so use it (see Part IV: The OKR Decision). Too many CEOs play the middle, letting side

....

3 AlixPartners, 9th Annual Private Equity Leadership Survey

projects blunt the impact of key priorities. Your teams will want to do *all* the things. Your job is to push them to tune out distractions and focus on what drives progress to the company's objectives.

- **Transparency:** Establish clear ownership of outcomes among your leadership team and provide the resources and support they need to succeed. Use regular cross-functional check-ins and dashboards to track execution and identify risks. Your job is to push the team to raise issues early and collaborate on solutions instead of letting gaps widen in silence.
- **Collaboration:** Cross-functional alignment doesn't happen on its own; you have to nurture it. Break silos between Sales, Marketing, Product, Customer Success, and Finance teams to drive efficient execution. Your job is to champion urgency by pushing your team to adopt scalable processes, tools, and alignment behaviors that support the company's growth strategy.

Adopting these values may feel uncomfortable at first because they can take some practice to master, but this is CEO work. No one else in the organization can align your leadership team at this level. That responsibility is yours alone.

HOW TO *NOT* SHOW WELL

Immediate results matter, but don't neglect the narrative that keeps your investors confident in the long-term strategy. Your PE firm may oversee dozens, if not hundreds, of portfolio companies. With busy schedules and frequent context-switching, it's on you to remind board investors of where the company stands within the long-term plan and how immediate results tie into the overall growth story.

Avoid withholding information. Just like with your leadership team, transparency here is key. Understand that investors have probably worked with hundreds of companies in some capacity and are experts at pattern recognition. They'll notice something's off, even if it isn't directly addressed. Own and frame issues clearly, raise them early, and frame them as part of the company's evolution. Problems are to be expected. Your ability to address them is what builds trust.

As CEO, you can't afford to be a step removed from the company's most important commercial decisions. Handing the four *Push* growth decisions over to your team without your direct involvement can quickly disconnect execution from *value creation.*

CEOs who fully delegate strategic decision-making risk deepening siloes and compounding inefficiency as misalignment worsens across functions. Even riskier is delegating strategic growth decisions entirely to a single trusted lieutenant. This introduces risk in two ways: First, it assumes they will make the right calls without your input (on decisions you will ultimately need to articulate and maybe defend). Second, it creates a structural vulnerability. If that leader leaves, you're left with a gap in both execution and strategic continuity. You must stay close, not only to reduce execution risk, but to ensure that growth remains intentional, cross-functional, and investor-aligned.

Now that you understand the pivotal role you play in connecting team execution to value creation, it's time to get started. The first, and most foundational, decision you'll make is the Ideal Customer Profile (ICP) Decision. Every growth lever in your value creation plan depends on knowing who you're targeting. Without a clear ICP, even the best growth strategies fail.

PART I

THE ICP DECISION

EXECUTIVE SUMMARY 3

THE IDEAL CUSTOMER PROFILE (ICP) DECISION DEFINED

Key Takeaways

- **Profitable Growth Starts with Your Customer**
  The ICP definition clarifies where to focus your team's efforts over the hold period to ensure growth is targeted not reactive.
- **Analysis Isn't Enough**
  Segmentation only defines your ICP. The real work starts once the team embeds that definition into their daily execution.
- **You Already Have the Data You Need**
  Much of what you need to define your ICP already exists in your CRM. Pair that data with insights from diligence to validate your go-forward strategy.
- **The CEO Needs to Participate**
  You don't need to run the analysis, but you do need to champion it, shape it, and ensure it gets executed across the functions.
- **You May Need to Outsource**
  The ICP definition is the cornerstone of your growth strategy. If your data is a mess or you lack in-house expertise, it's worth the investment to bring in outside help.

Why the ICP Decision Matters

The ICP Decision answers one of the most important questions you'll face as CEO post-investment: *Who is our best customer for this next phase of growth?* A well-defined ICP serves as a strategic anchor. It aligns your team on who to target, where to allocate resources and how to prioritize your roadmap. Because it uses your own customer data, it's also one of the most accessible ways to validate the "market" component of product-market fit.

However, understanding the ICP alone is not enough. Once it is defined, the CEO must push the team to take action on those learnings with commercial execution and an aligned product roadmap.

A well-defined ICP:

- Translates the Total Addressable Market (TAM) into targetable customers,
- Aligns Product, Marketing, Sales, and Customer Success with one view of the customer, and
- Validates market-related value creation levers before scaling spend.

3

THE IDEAL CUSTOMER PROFILE (ICP) DECISION DEFINED

THE IDEAL CUSTOMER PROFILE (ICP) Decision answers the question of *Who is our best customer for this next phase of growth?* Generally, an ICP identifies your highest-value account segments: the accounts most likely to buy, expand, and renew. They create a strategic anchor for team focus, resource allocation, and roadmap prioritization. This chapter introduces the concept of an ideal customer profile, explains your unique role as CEO in developing and executing on one, and arms you with the common traps to avoid.

ICPs are commonly mistaken for personas, but these are two different things. An ICP defines account-level firmographic traits like industry, company size, or technographic traits like platforms in use, while personas describe buyer-level demographic traits like job title and seniority. Personas exist within ICP accounts and represent the roles you need to influence to win a deal like a champion, decision-maker, or user. In the Push Order of Operations, you first need to decide on the characteristics of your ICP account segments before drilling down into the personas in those accounts. This order enables you to define the needs, challenges, and objections of the key personas *based* on their company profile. The needs and challenges of selling to the CTO of a $50M healthcare company are going to be different from selling to the CTO of a $50M retail company. In this example, the CTO is the *"persona"* and the $50M healthcare company is the *"ICP."* You can't properly define your key personas until you first decide on the ICP accounts to target.

The ICP Decision isn't a one-time event. It's a strategic decision you'll revisit as the company evolves, particularly after a round of investment. Revalidating your ICP at this stage ensures that the "high-value" segments your team has historically targeted are still the right ones to get you from here to the next exit. Post-close, your job as CEO is to confirm whether those segments are big enough, aligned-to-the-roadmap enough, and valuable enough to unlock the Total Addressable Market (TAM) opportunities laid out in the investment thesis. Segmentation analysis is how you confirm this (see Figure 8).

Segmentation analysis uses your customer and prospect data to pinpoint the firmographic and technographic traits that define your best-fit customer accounts. It's one of the most accessible ways to validate the "market" component of product-market fit, because everything you need already exists in your CRM. By pairing that analysis with your investor's market research from diligence (such as customer calls or third-party market studies), you can identify a go-forward ICP based on today's market *and* what has worked for you historically.

A well-defined ICP does three things for you.

1. **It translates the Total Addressable Market (TAM) into targetable traits.** Market studies size the potential of a market, your ICP definition is where you start that expansion. Sales and Marketing can only prospect at scale by targeting traits available in data platforms. To be effective, they will need to understand which traits to target in those platforms. Without that clarity, teams struggle to source pipeline consistently or efficiently.
2. **It aligns Product, Marketing, Sales, and Customer Success to build, sell, and serve the same customer.** Without an ICP anchor, companies evolve in fragmented ways. Product builds to the wrong use cases, Sales and Marketing struggle to position on

FIGURE 8: Total Addressable Market (TAM)

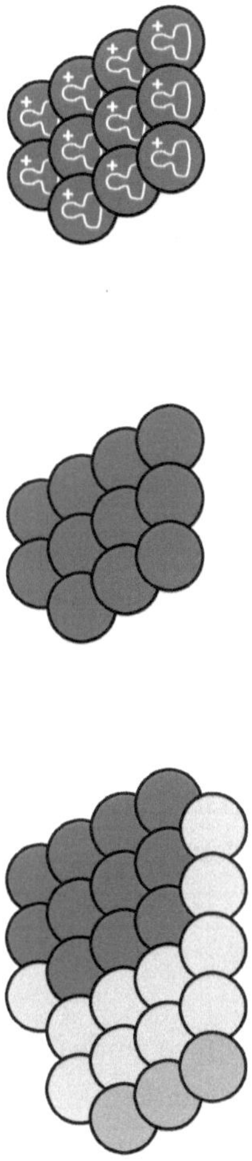

	TAM	ICP	PERSONA
What it represents	The Total Addressable Market revenue potential modeled in the investment thesis.	Your highest-value account segments, most likely to buy, expand, and renew.	Buyer roles within ICP accounts.
Who defines it	Investor	CEO	GTM teams
Question it answers	Is the market big enough to provide a return on our investment?	Who is our best customer for this phase of growth?	Who do we need to influence to win the deal?
When it's set	During diligence	Post-close / revisit as needed	After ICP is defined.

value, and Customer Success is left trying to renew customers that were never really a good fit for the product to begin with.

3. **It validates your value creation growth levers before you commit significant spend.** CEOs who skip the ICP Decision often misallocate resources, wasting budget on channels or targets that don't convert, misaligning product investment, and creating churn risk. A clear ICP ensures team-wide alignment about whom to target, how to message, and how to deliver a product that sells. Validating the go-forward ideal customer profile in the context of the 100-Day Plan gives you the opportunity to ensure you're targeting the right customers, based on your own data, before directing your team to execute.

WHY THE ICP DECISION COMES FIRST

You are starting this growth journey by focusing on your best customer. The ICP Decision translates the investor's market study and growth thesis into account traits that can be targeted by your team. Whether the investment strategy involves organic growth in core markets or expansion into adjacent segments, your ICP directs go-to-market (GTM) activity where it has the highest chance of success. That clarity reduces wasted effort, increases efficiency, and prepares your teams to execute confidently.

ROLE OF THE CEO

For many CEOs, the ICP Decision is the first opportunity to guide their cross-functional team as one unit through a maturity transformation. Although ICP definition is critical to growth, many teams under $100M haven't run a full segmentation analysis before. Fewer still have connected ICP definition to downstream execution. As CEO, you won't be in the weeds of execution, but you do play a critical role in facilitating momentum and focusing the team on the bigger picture. In this way, your role has a few dimensions.

1. **Champion:** Set this as priority for your leadership team. Your team still needs to hit this quarter's numbers, but don't let short-term

pressure delay foundational work. You may need to de-prioritize lower-impact projects to free up capacity. They need to keep the lights on, but this process will help you reset the direction of your company for the next three to five years.

2. **Participate:** CEO participation is lightweight but essential, particularly in shaping the initial hypothesis formed in the ICP Workshop (see Chapter 4). You're not driving the day-to-day work, but your perspective ensures the process aligns with the Value Creation Plan and where you want the company to be at exit.
3. **Resource:** Appoint a project lead. This can be someone from your Revenue Operations (RevOps), Sales, Marketing, or Product teams. Depending on the skills of your team and the completeness of your data, you may need to find an outsourced partner to help with analysis or data prep. Ask your investor if an analyst or Operating Partner is available to support the work. If not, they may have a short list of proven vendors who've done this successfully for other portfolio companies. It shows well to ask.
4. **Upskill:** You don't have to teach the project lead how to run a segmentation analysis, but encourage them to self-learn with examples, books or webinars. Your investor may have sanitized examples to share or a peer from another portfolio company to connect with your project lead. Ask your project lead to prepare a brief explainer slide for use during the kick-off to align the stakeholder group on the process. This not only aligns the team but serves as a gut check for you; it's how you'll know your lead has learned enough to take on the project effectively.

COMMON CEO MISTAKE: ASSUMING ANALYSIS IS THE GOAL

Teams often feel a sense of accomplishment just getting through the segmentation analysis and defining the ICP segments. Beware of thinking you are done once the ICP is defined. Some teams fall into the trap of assuming the analysis was the goal. They may roadshow the segmentation findings across the organization, solicit feedback, foster debate, and assume those sessions were the "roll-out" of the ICP, but this wasn't just an exercise in understanding the buyer.

You set out to validate the ICP so you could align the product roadmap for improved sales and retention, organize your sales territories to boost quota attainment, and direct prospect targeting to improve marketing ROI. If you stop short of executing on the ICP definitions, you won't see these improvements. If no concrete actions are put in place to embed the ICP definition into commercial execution, then you've only spent a lot of effort on surfacing some neat findings.

WHEN TO OUTSOURCE

Three things need to be in place to successfully complete an analysis that can define an ICP:

1. An informed hypothesis of your target customer
2. Access to customer data (even if imperfect)
3. Someone capable of analyzing the data

If your CRM is a mess or you don't have a strong analyst available in-house, then you need to bring in outside help. There are plenty of experienced vendors and service partners who can support both the data prep and the analysis. This is an area where it's better to invest in third-party support than to skip the process.

At the time of this writing, expect to spend between $30k–$200k. depending on the complexity of your product and the state of your data. If your CRM is at least 60% complete (i.e., not blank) with usable data, then you may only need to source a third-party analyst. If your data is less than 60% complete or usable, then you will need to invest more with a partner who can first improve your data before they can engage in the analysis. Either way, start your search by asking your investor whether they have an in-house analyst or Operating Partner available to help. Some PE firms offer this kind of support gratis to their portfolio companies.

If you are unsure whether to outsource, use the sample vendor brief in

FIGURE 9: Example Vendor Brief

Vendor Brief: ICP Definiton and Segmentation Analysis

About The Company:
A $45M ARR vertical SaaS company serving mid-market and enterprise e-commerce retailers in key high-SKU verticals like fashion and automotive. In business for 11 years, with deep expertise in its category and a sticky customer base.

Project Goals:

- Deepen penetration in the North American market (currently ~15% penetrated)
- Scale early traction in Europe by identifying high-fit customer segments and territories for expansion

Needs:

- Define ICP tiers (A and B) based on historical deal size, sales velocity, and win rates
- Identify key prospecting attributes: firmographics (vertical, employee size), technographics (platform licenses), and behavioral markers
- Recommend territories based on A/B account mix and performance
- Identify top prospecting channels: events, associations, channel partners, etc.
- Identify gaps in CRM data and recommend next steps to improve data hygiene and completeness

Available Data:

- Historical CRM data (pipeline, win/loss, segmentation, revenue)
- Enriched firmographic and technographic data
- Access to top customers and internal SMEs for interviews

Timeline:

- 6-8 week project window, including discovery, analysis, validation, and final recommendations

Figure 9 to assess whether you have the internal resources to execute this project.

Regardless of whether you outsource the analysis, you still play a critical role as CEO. You are accountable for ensuring the ICP aligns with your investment thesis, reflects business realities, and can be operationalized across the company.

Now that you understand what the ICP is and why it matters, you'll take the first step and lead your team to make the ICP Decision. In the next chapter, you'll learn how to organize and run the ICP Workshop and how to guide your team through the analysis that will define your go-forward Ideal Customer Profile.

AI Fragmented the Market

Bookings for a $35M verticalized back-office company had become unpredictable and the team started to miss forecast. With the advent of artificial intelligence (AI), a growing number of smaller point solution competitors began flooding the market. Customer Acquisition Cost (CAC) rose as these new competitors drove up the cost for high-converting lead sources. Market fragmentation led to lost deals as features became commoditized and differentiation became harder to prove. The CEO increased marketing's budget to maintain lead volume, but worsening lead-to-opportunity conversion rates rendered the spend unprofitable. Sales reps were missing quotas and morale dipped as the company struggled to hit its growth targets.

What the CEO Heard from the Team

- "CPLs (Cost-Per-Leads) are being driven up by competitors."
- "We're seeing more competition in every deal."
- "We're losing on price."

What the CEO Saw in the Data

- Lower LTV:CAC from newer customer cohorts
- Shrinking pipeline coverage (the amount of pipeline available for reps to close in a given time period)
- Declining win rates in core verticals

Solution

The market dynamics had shifted, and it was time to revisit whether the company could still hit its plan by continuing to focus on their existing ICP alone or whether there were adjacent segments ready for expansion. The CEO knew they needed to revisit the ICP definitions to confirm. They gathered leaders from Product, Sales, Marketing, and Customer Success. The team then used their hypothesized traits from the workshop to guide the analysis of their CRM data. By using these traits as their anchor, they surfaced three adjacent markets that had the lowest churn rates, the best win rates, the highest deal size, and the longest customer tenure among their existing customer and prospect accounts. The CEO enlisted the investor to supplement the analysis with competitive intel.

The team ranked the adjacent markets and moved up feature development to support the first one. Sales and Marketing worked together to identify accounts to target, value messaging to support, and territories to assign. While Product worked through their sprints, Sales and Marketing prepared for launch with rep training and campaign planning. The CEO championed the roadmap shift with investors and leveraged the board's relationships for introductions to new strategic partners. The CEO and their team stayed hyper-focused on the new launch, leveraging OKRs (see Part IV) to manage the deliverables between the teams and communicate progress back to the board. It took two quarters post-launch to achieve plan revenue for the first time in almost a year.

EXECUTIVE SUMMARY 4

HOW CEOS MAKE THE ICP DECISION

Key Takeaways

- **Your ICP Definition Grounds GTM Execution**
  It anchors Product, Sales, Marketing, and Customer Success on a singular understanding of the target customer.
- **The ICP Workshop Ensures Adoption Later**
  Engaging Sales, Marketing, Customer Success, and Product leaders early brings critical insights to the surface and builds buy-in for execution later.
- **Analysis Yields a Defensible Target**
  Use your CRM data to run a segmentation analysis and validate the team's instincts about what makes a good customer using metrics like median deal size, sales cycle length, and churn.
- **Do Not Default to Average Deal Size**
  Model both average and median selling price to ensure your team is forecasting on a true predictable number.
- **Align with Your Board Before Execution**
  Quickly discuss the ICP definition with your investors to confirm alignment with the Value Creation Plan before directing your team to embed it into their daily practices.

Chapter 4 Deliverables

By the end of this chapter, you should have:

- Hypothesized Traits and Data Hygiene Guide
- Enriched CRM Dataset
- Segmentation Analysis
- ICP Definitions for Tiered Segments
- Company Benchmarks on Key Metrics
- Board Alignment to the ICP

Why Making the ICP Decision Matters

The ICP definition is how CEOs translate the TAM from the market study into an actionable go-to-market plan. It's the foundation for every other growth lever, from campaign targeting and territory design to sales enablement and product roadmap. By starting with a cross-functional workshop and validating the team's instincts with real data, you reduce friction during execution and gain buy-in from your leadership team early.

Modeling ICP segments using metrics like deal size, win rate, and churn gives you a data-backed view of where *achievable* growth is most likely to come from. ICP tiers like A, B, C, and D help coordinate your teams to move faster on landing top accounts.

By aligning the final ICP definition with your board, you minimize risk of wasted execution effort later. This checkpoint builds confidence in the strategy before go-to-market investments are made and ensures the path forward reflects the growth thesis behind the deal.

4

HOW CEOS MAKE THE ICP DECISION

DURATION: 51 DAYS FOR DECISION (DAYS 1–51)

THE ICP DECISION comes first in the Push Order of Operations as it sets the strategic direction for the rest of your growth decisions. This chapter guides you through the five steps required to define your go-forward ICP definition and align it with your board before execution begins. The entire process takes 51 days, with 40 of those days reserved for analysis.

Making the ICP Decision takes five steps:

1. **ICP Workshop:** Hypothesize the account traits that define high-value customers today.
2. **Prepare & Append Data:** Ensure CRM data is complete and ready for analysis.
3. **Conduct Segmentation Analysis:** Track data patterns to identify high-value buyer segments.
4. **Define the ICP:** Summarize findings to train and align internal teams.
5. **Present ICP to the Board:** Ensure alignment with the investment thesis before execution begins.

By starting the process with a quick cross-functional workshop, you solicit insights from the stakeholders who know your customers best and encourage adoption in the later execution steps as teams see their insights reflected in the output. Step 1 walks you through how to get started.

STEP 1: ICP WORKSHOP

Owner: *CEO,* **Duration:** *1–2 Hours (Day 1)*

Every *Push* decision starts with a team workshop. These workshops surface expertise and insights from your leaders and are the secret to aligning them behind transforming the subsequent team process. For the ICP Workshop, you'll kick off with leaders from Sales, Marketing, Customer Success, and Product (your customer-facing teams), and workshop the account traits that they think indicate your highest-value, lowest-churn customers. These hypothesized traits will serve as your compass for the segmentation analysis that follows.

Expect to undergo some form of this trait-hypothesis workshop whether you are insourcing or outsourcing the analysis. If insourcing, use the templates and process provided here as a starting point. If outsourcing, the vendor probably has a framework and process they prefer to use.

Because the participants all have a unique relationship with the buyer, the discussion and debate from this exercise can uncover insights that weren't widely understood. Do not skip over disagreements or rush the discussion. A well-facilitated session raises disagreements and addresses challenges in the room (which leads to better adoption later). When you encourage open discussion, the ICP Workshop can be great for bonding the leadership team around a singular view of the customer.

Before the session, secure permission from your investor to share the market study from diligence with your team. The market study is what your investor used to size the Total Addressable Market (TAM), your position in that market, and the competitive landscape. This third-party research provides a broad market perspective and can validate some of the key attributes or traits that come out of the workshop. Sharing the study as pre-work equips the team with the market-level context needed for an informed discussion in the room.

ICP Workshop Agenda

The ICP Workshop is the most lightweight of the four Push Workshops, typically lasting about an hour when the right participants are in the room. While some teams may be aligning with the specifics of what makes a good customer for the first time, it is usually a low-friction conversation.

This is one of the few workshops where the CEO can choose to lead or delegate facilitation to any leader from the group. To ensure the hypothesis covers the entire customer lifecycle, attendees should include leaders from Product, Sales, Marketing, Customer Success, Revenue Operations, and your Product Marketing lead (if that role exists). *You* also need to participate in this workshop. Defining the ICP will anchor all subsequent growth decisions and materially affect your company over the long-term.

The output of this session is a list of account traits that serve as the foundation for the segmentation analysis that follows. In this workshop, you'll address four key topics, which will become your agenda.

1. **Align on Objectives:** Kick off with a quick explanation of why the team is coming together to define or validate their understanding of the ideal customer. For context, raise any findings from the market study or the Value Creation Plan that the team may need to know.
2. **Suggest Traits:** Gather stakeholders to answer, *What traits typically indicate a high-value or a sticky customer?* (e.g., vertical, geography, install base). Capture answers live in real time for all of the attendees to see.
3. **Hypothesize Segments:** Specify what "good" looks like for each trait. For example, if the team identified "Vertical" as a key trait, which verticals specifically do they think are highest-value (e.g., "Vertical = healthcare or retail")?
4. **Assess Data Readiness:** Estimate how ready your CRM data is to analyze these traits. Assess general data quality (is the data generally reliable?) and completeness (roughly how many blanks exist?) for each trait and determine whether the team has access to or can acquire a third-party data source to enrich the fields.

Use the agenda provided in Figure 10 to address these four key topics. The group's answers to these questions will give your RevOps lead clear direction in terms of what data to collect before the analysis and codifies the starting place for your analyst.

Nominate someone to write down/record the answers to these questions and by the end of the session, you will have a list of the key traits to confirm or append in your CRM along with an initial ICP hypothesis for your analyst to validate during segmentation (see Figure 11).

Now that you've aligned with a working hypothesis of what a good customer looks like, it's time to prepare and append the data that will validate or challenge that assumption.

FIGURE 10: ICP Workshop Agenda

Duration	Agenda	Owner	Attendees
Pre-Work	Read the Market Study from diligence	All	
5 min.	**Align on Objectives:** What market do we want to penetrate further?	CEO	• Head of Product • Head of Sales • Head of Marketing • Head of Customer Success • Product Marketing Lead • RevOps Lead
20 min.	**Suggest Traits:** What attributes or traits do our highest-value customers in this market share (i.e., specific verticals, geographies, employee count)?		
20 min.	**Hypothesize Segments:** For each trait, what does a high-value customer generally look like (e.g., geography = North America, verticals = credit unions and banks, employee count = 200–2000)?		
15 min.	**Assess Data Readiness:** For each trait listed, how complete and usable is the data in our CRM? Is an enrichment platform available to build out the data?		

STEP 2: PREPARE & APPEND DATA

Owner: *RevOps Leader,* **Duration:** *7 Days (Days 2–9)*

Armed with hypothesized traits, or attributes, from the workshop, it's time to prepare the CRM data for analysis. This involves cleaning up fields and enriching incomplete or outdated data using third-party platforms. Appending this data to your CRM for segmentation is also the first meaningful step your team will take toward improved data hygiene in *The Push Framework.*

In this exercise, appending data serves two purposes: It ensures the data is usable for segmentation analysis and prepares your CRM for upcoming account scoring (see Chapter 5, Step 5). Without this step, your team risks working with incomplete or unreliable data, which can lead to inaccurate findings from the analysis and a limited pool of potential opportunities for your Sales and Marketing teams to target later.

FIGURE 11: Hypothesized ICP Traits: Example from Workshop

Segment Detail		Data Readiness				
Pre-Work	**High-Value Customer (team hypothesis)**	**Current Data Availability**	**Data Quality**	**Level Of Effort To Append Data**	**Data Enrichment Source**	**Notes**
Industry	Financial Energy Healthcare	90%	OK	Low	Zoominfo	Data API in place; Data not validated
Employee Count	200-2000	10%	Poor	Low	Zoominfo	Data available; not yet appended
Geography	North America	100%	Good	Low	Zoominfo	Data API in place; validated by Reps
Partner Types	Referral (Financial Advisors)	75%	Good	High	Zoominfo	Existing partner in CRM

Your data will never be perfect, but the more blanks or inaccuracies in your CRM fields, the less useful your analysis will be. You can run a meaningful segmentation analysis when 75% or more of your CRM fields are complete, and a lighter-weight analysis with more than 60% completeness. If the fields you need for analysis are less than 60% complete, then pause and prioritize data hygiene; you will need to append and clean the missing fields first. Once your database is in a usable state, you're ready to move on to analysis.

Before moving on to analysis, run a quick data validation exercise. Encourage each functional leader (Marketing, Sales, Customer Success) to review five to 10 customer records and confirm the enriched data aligns with known customer information. Focus on critical attributes like geography, industry, and employee count.

Once your data is validated and as complete as it can be, you're ready for analysis.

STEP 3: CONDUCT SEGMENTATION ANALYSIS

Owner: *RevOps Leader,* **Duration:** *40 Days (Days 10–50)*

With the data ready and an understanding of the hypothesized traits in hand, your analyst is ready to track patterns and identify the segments that will define your ICP. Focus on metrics like deal size (typically tracked as ARR), churn rates, and sales cycle times to determine which traits are most closely correlated with highest deal size, lowest churn, and fastest sales cycle accounts.

The trait combinations that surface will help you form your ICP segments. A trait is a single attribute, like industry or employee count, while a segment is a group of accounts that share a specific combination of traits (see Figure 12). This would look like all healthcare and retail accounts that have fewer than 1,000 employees may fit under a SMB segment. In this example, the combination of traits (vertical plus employee count) defines the segment (SMB).

These ICP segments are your ideal customers. While you may still sell to accounts outside these segments, you will direct Sales and Marketing to proactively target and spend dollars and effort on going after these

FIGURE 12: Data Fields for Segmentation Analysis

CRM Export Type	Data Fields
Account Data	Account Name, Industry, Created Date, Closed Date, Country/State/Province, Unique ID, Deal Size (ARR Start, ARR End), Products Owned, Renewal Date, Customer Tier (SMB, Mid-Market, Enterprise), Customer Health Score (optional), Churn Reason, Sub-Industry, Employee Count, Rep Name, Contacts (Job Title), Lead Source, Partner Name, Parent Account (optional), Account Rep, Attributes identified in the workshop (Step 1)
Opportunity Data	Opportunity Name, Stage, Probability %,Opportunity Value (Amount), Days in Stage (or Created Date and Close Date), Lead Source, Unique ID, Reason for Win/Loss, Product Name, Account Rep, Attributes Identified in the workshop (Step 1)

highest-value prospects. Using time or money to target outside of your ICP segments is a distraction for the team and the budget.

Analysis that overlooks these four critical factors can lead to misleading incomplete analysis:

- deal size (selling price)
- sales cycle time
- customer lifetime (or how long a customer is active, counted in years)
- churn rates

At a minimum, your analysis should include these metrics. How accounts rank against these metrics will determine who is "ideal" and who is not.

Segmentation analysis requires specialized skills. If you have a skilled analyst in RevOps, Finance, Marketing, or Product, they may be able to run this analysis, but if internal capacity or capability is lacking, this is an area worth outsourcing. A dedicated analyst can often complete this work within four to six weeks of getting the data.

FIGURE 13: The Language of Segmentation

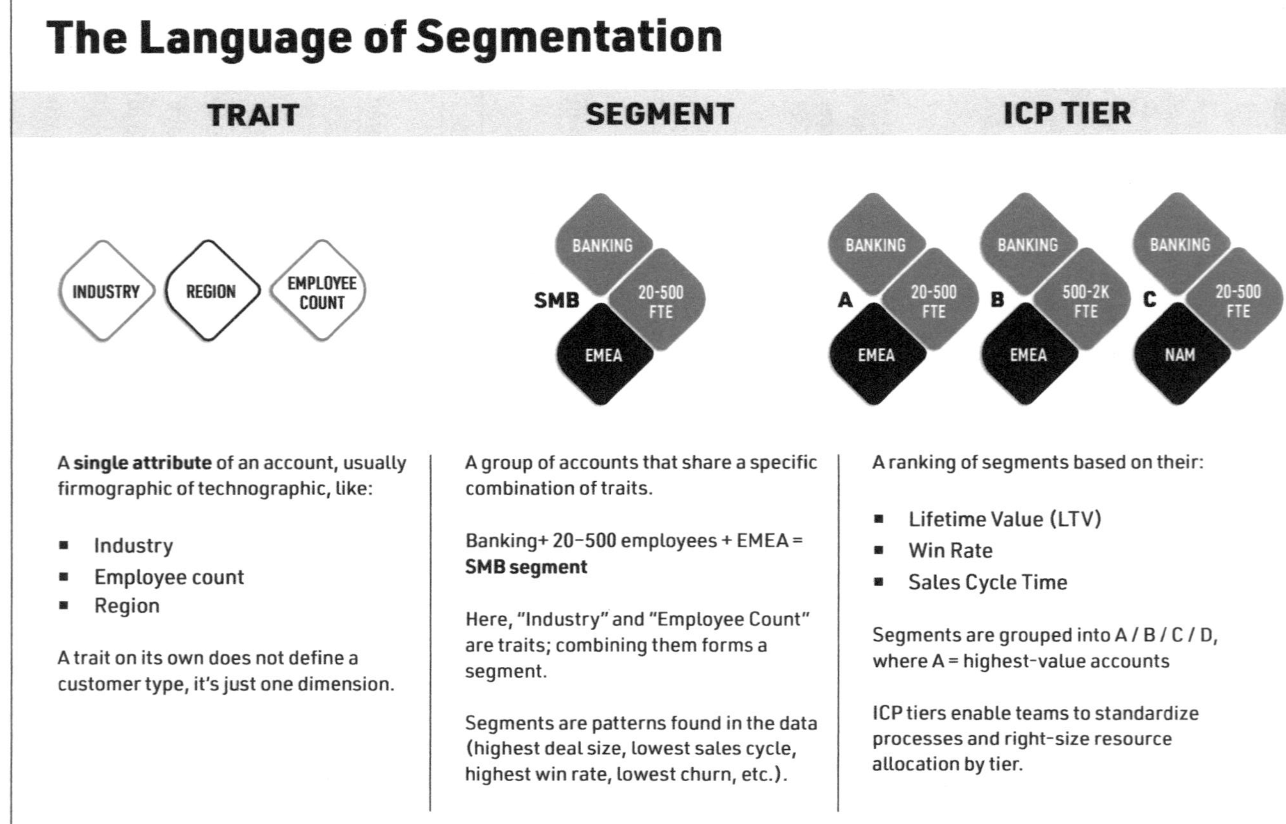

Common CEO Mistake: Defaulting to Average Deal Size

One of the most common traps CEOs fall into is forecasting an unsustainable average deal size. This analysis is your opportunity to be clear about the true *predictable* selling price for an account by verifying the median deal size of your segments.

Median deal size is calculated by ordering all like closed-won deals by deal size and selecting the middle one. It identifies the midpoint. Unlike the average (which sums all deal values and divides by the total number of deals), the median avoids the distortion that comes from landing one really big deal that would skew the number.

Generally, the median deal size is a truer reflection of a typical deal size and a more reliable input for forecasting, territory planning, and quota setting. Using the average deal size is fine, as long as it is similar to the median. However, if your average deal size and your median deal size have a large delta, then forecasting on that average can inadvertently set your reps up for a miss right out of the gate. In that case, you've forecasted that reps will land some *unusual accounts* to make their targets. And we aren't trying to land unusual accounts; we're trying to land *ideal accounts*. For some teams, identifying the median deal size is one of the most important, and sometimes the most sobering, findings to emerge from this analysis.

As part of your segmentation analysis, direct your analyst to model both the average and the median deal sizes for your segments. You'll use median deal size as the baseline for the final ICP tiers but reviewing both metrics helps you understand which the right number is to use in forecasting.

From Traits to Segments to ICP Tiers

Once your analyst has identified the combination of traits that yield the largest median deal size, shortest sales cycle, highest win rate, and lowest churn, distinct patterns will emerge in the data. These patterns will define the segments that you will later group accounts into (see Chapter 5, Step 5). Segments often, but not always, cluster by company size (Enterprise, Mid-Market, SMB), vertical (Retail, Healthcare, Financial Services) or geography (NAM, EU, APAC).

FIGURE 14: ICP Tiers Example

Tiers	Segments	Traits or Attributes	Median Deal Size	Sales Cycle	Win Rate	Customer Lifetime (Years)	Lifetime Value (LTV) Potential	Current Customer Examples
A	US Mid-Market	Industry (Retail) Employee Count (101-1000) Region (NAM)	$30K	90 Days	30%	5	$150K	Name 1 Name 2 Name 3
B	US SMB	Industry (Retail) Employee Count (11-50) Region (NAM)	$23K	45 Days	28%	3	$69K	Name 1 Name 2 Name 3
C	APAC SMB	Industry (Retail) Employee Count (1-10) Region (APAC)	$15K	15 Days	45%	2	$30K	Name 1 Name 2 Name 3
D	De-Prioritize	All Others	–	–	–	–	–	Name 1 Name 2 Name 3

The next step is to tier these segments by potential Lifetime Value (LTV). For this exercise, LTV is calculated simply as:

Median Deal Size x Customer Lifetime (in years)

This simplified LTV modeling isn't meant to replace detailed revenue planning; for this exercise, it's a simple tool for ranking segments based on their value potential. Inputs like win rate and sales cycle time are layered in to help prioritize which segments offer the greatest efficiency and upside. Segments with the strongest performance in these metrics in combination become your "A" accounts or your top ICP tier. Lower-performing segments are classified as "B," "C," or even "D" tiers, with D-tier accounts typically deprioritized or even labeled as "Do Not Sell" for some companies (see Figure 14).

To bring your ICP tiers to life, include examples of current customers who match the defined traits of each segment. This not only validates the logic of your segmentation but also helps teams visualize who belongs in each tier and why. If possible, use real names that the teams will recognize. By the end of this analysis, you should have a clear understanding of the combination of traits that make up your most valuable customer segments, as well as your company's benchmarks for deal size, win rate, sales cycle time, customer lifetime years, and LTV against those segments.

With your ICP segments defined and validated with real customer examples, the next step is to align those target account profiles with the board.

STEP 4: ICP BOARD ALIGNMENT

Owner: *CEO,* **Duration:** *1 Hour (Day 51)*

This step is quick but serves as a key checkpoint to ensure that your plans tie back to the investment thesis before shifting your team into execution.

Most investors value proactive alignment sessions when it clarifies how the CEO plans to execute against the Value Creation Plan. They want to understand and buy into thesis-related decisions because they may need to explain or even defend this rationale to their investment committee at some later point. The objective of this step is to validate that the ICP definition aligns with the investor expectations before directing your team to execute. This check will also help you probe for board relationships that may help you expand farther into your market.

Key questions to address in your alignment session with your board investors include:

- *Do our findings align with the investment thesis?*
- *How do these findings affect the M&A pipeline?*
- *Are there strategic partnerships or relationships the board can help facilitate?*
- *Should we add a board advisor with relationships or expertise in the prioritized segments?*
- *Do the findings suggest potential for a particular type of strategic investment buyer in the long term?*

FIGURE 15: ICP Board Alignment Agenda

Duration	Agenda	Owner	Attendees
5 min.	**Overview of the Analysis:** Briefly explain the methodology and key questions guiding the analysis.	CEO	Board
5 min.	**Segmentation Findings:** Present an executive summary of the data.		
20 min.	**ICP and Account Tiers:** Walk through the ICP attributes and the A/B account tiers.		
30 min.	**CEO Discussion Topics:** • Alignment with the investment thesis. • Opportunities for strategic buyers. • Impact on the M&A pipeline. • Partnership opportunities and board support.		

If you have a scheduled board meeting, add this to the agenda (see Figure 15). If not, request a one-off meeting to discuss the findings. Provide the segmentation analysis, key takeaways, and ICP tier definitions as a pre-read.

Once your ICP is clearly defined and board-aligned, it's time to embed those learnings into your team's daily practices. Chapter 5 walks you through how to operationalize the ICP across your commercial teams.

EXECUTIVE SUMMARY 5

HOW CEOS EXECUTE THE ICP DECISION

Key Takeaways

- **Account Scoring Operationalizes Your ICP**
  Use the ICP traits from your segmentation analysis to build CRM-based account scoring logic. Prioritize A and B tier accounts to focus rep time, improve quota attainment, and prepare for territory planning and outbound targeting.

- **Account Scoring ≠ Lead Scoring**
  Account scoring happens at the company level (in your CRM) to guide Sales, Marketing, and Customer Success efforts. Lead scoring happens in your Marketing Automation Platform (MAP) and prioritizes leads for sales to qualify.

- **You Sell to People, Not Accounts**
  Personas and positioning help you engage the champions, decision-makers, and users in key accounts. Pair personas with positioning that clearly answers, *Why us?* and is personalized to the unique challenges of the buyer's role.

- **Use AI for Account Scoring Only after the Logic is Set**
  If your CRM fields are clean and your ICP logic is defined, AI tools can accelerate scoring at scale. However, AI can't fix bad logic or missing data. Treat it as an accelerant, not a shortcut.

- **The CEO Orchestrates Execution**
  Your job is not to map the account scores or write the personas, but to prioritize the work, reinforce coordination, and remove roadblocks.

ICP Execution Deliverables

By the end of this chapter, you should have:

- CRM-Based Account Scoring
- Validated Buyer Personas
- Positioning Statements
- Persona-Based GPT Instructions

Why Executing the ICP Matters

By embedding your ICP definition into account scoring, personas, and positioning, you align the commercial team with whom to target, how to target, and what to say. *This sets the foundation for the next three decisions.*

The steps laid out in this chapter improve sales velocity and overall conversion by taking some of the guesswork and subjectivity out of selling. They also take the first steps toward future activities, such as territory planning and campaign design (see Chapter 14, Steps 11 and 12).

Operationalizing the ICP in this phase strengthens the cross-team coordination that is the hallmark of go-to-market maturity. You will build on this alignment with each decision in this book. If these steps are skipped or done poorly, CEOs may see reps revert to cherry-picking deals, Marketing run campaigns that don't convert, and product ship features that don't resonate.

5

HOW CEOS EXECUTE THE ICP DECISION

DURATION: 14 DAYS FOR EXECUTION (DAYS 52–66)

ONCE YOUR ICP definition is set, execution can begin. This chapter shows you how to direct your teams to embed the ICP into your core go-to-market structure. Over the next two weeks, RevOps and Marketing will operationalize the ICP through account scoring, persona development, and positioning. In parallel, Product begins roadmap planning against the same ICP.

This coordinated burst of activity ensures that your commercial teams aren't just aware of the ICP but are using it. The accounts you prioritize, the buyers you target, and the messaging you use will all originate in the steps laid out in this execution phase. These first execution steps shape how your teams will engage and convert ICP accounts going forward and set your teams up to execute on future activities like territory planning (see Chapter 14, Step 11) and campaign development (see Chapter 14, Step 12) in a coordinated fashion. By ensuring these embeds are in place now, you avoid misalignment later.

CEO ROLE

During the ICP execution phase, your job is to manage the speed of execution. That includes prioritizing the ICP execution milestones, resourcing your teams appropriately, and removing roadblocks, all while reinforcing collaboration among functions. The ICP execution milestones for this are:

- **Step 5: Account Scoring**—owned by RevOps
- **Step 6: Personas and Positioning**—owned by Marketing
- *(In parallel: Roadmap Planning—owned by Product)*

Let's start with Step 5.

STEP 5: ACCOUNT SCORING

Owner: *RevOps Leader,* **Duration:** *14 Days (Days 52–66)*

Account scoring tiers the accounts, both incoming and existing, in your CRM based on the segments you defined in segmentation. Account scoring removes the guesswork and subjectivity from the rep's day-to-day because the system automates serving them the highest-value accounts to work. This automation focuses the rep's time on the highest-value accounts most likely to convert, expand, and renew.

Account scoring is a powerful tool. It helps load-balance your rep's time, positioning them better to hit their quotas; gives Customer Success teams a way to prioritize customer outreach to uncover signals for cross-selling or upselling opportunities more efficiently; and helps Marketing prioritize messaging and targeting to priority accounts in alignment with Sales and Customer Success. High-scoring accounts reflect the ICP segments, or combination of traits, you identified in Chapter 4.

Do not confuse account scoring with lead scoring. Account scoring happens in the CRM and scores based on company or account level traits; it drives prioritization of accounts for Sales and Customer Success to work, and is used for rep targeting and territory development. Lead scoring, which comes later in the Push Order of Operations (but happens first in the buying cycle), takes place as automation in the marketing automation platform (MAP) at the lead level and helps Marketing prioritize which leads to route to sales for qualification and follow-up. Lead scoring logic is dependent on account scoring and therefore will come later in the build, in Chapter 8.

Account scoring can be implemented with basic CRM functionality or manually (without automation) using a spreadsheet. It requires minimal setup and resources to implement: You just need a person to build out the logic for the account score and implement it into your CRM. This tends to fall under the RevOps function. If that role doesn't exist at your company, this is an easy and generally low-cost project to outsource, as long as you've already completed the segmentation analysis. Assume three to five days to set up the scoring logic and an additional week to test and validate the logic.

CEO TL;DR

Account Scoring Implementation Steps

1. **Define Scoring Logic:** Use ICP tiers from Chapter 4 to map the logic for scoring accounts in your CRM.
2. **Build in CRM or Spreadsheet:** Implement scoring logic in your CRM or against a static list of accounts (if manual).
3. **Validate and Test:** Validate scores on a sample of accounts to ensure they align with real-world behaviors.

How to Implement Account Scoring (Instructions for Your Team)

Before building account scoring into the CRM, your RevOps lead first must map the logic behind the scoring system. Follow these steps to build a simple, scalable model aligned with your ICP (see Figure 16).

Assign the Total Max Score

Start by setting a total max score. This is the highest possible score an account can earn when all trait scores are summed. It sets the ceiling for an A Account.

1. **Assign the Max Score for Each Trait**
   Carry over the ICP traits you identified in Chapter 4 (e.g., Geography, Industry, Employee Count) and assign a maximum allowable score

AI FOR ACCOUNT SCORING

Some CRMs offer AI-powered scoring features that can simplify this process, but successful AI scoring requires that the foundations are solid. To use AI scoring effectively, your team needs:

- Clean and complete data fields on the traits being scored (see Chapter 4, Step 2)
- Defined account scoring logic (see Step 5) to inform or override the model
- A validation step to test whether the AI outputs align with real-world behavior

AI here is not a shortcut. It can accelerate scoring at scale, but it won't fix bad inputs or misaligned logic.

to each trait based on its importance. Not all traits are equally predictive of ICP fit. Unless you have a data-savvy RevOps lead and a clear statistical model, skip formal percentage weighting and instead, assign higher max scores to more predictive traits. This method is easier to implement than percentage weighting, and still reflects the relative importance of each trait.

2. **Assign Selection Scores**
   Each trait will have multiple selections available (e.g., different industries, geographies, or employee ranges). Assign scores to each value based on how well it aligns with your ICP tiers from Chapter 4. For example, if *Fashion & Apparel* was identified as an A-tier industry, it should receive the maximum score allowed for the industry trait.
3. **Assign the Score Ranges to ICP Tiers**
   Once you've scored all traits and totaled the account score, group accounts into ICP tiers based on those totals. A simple starting

point might look like:

   a. 80–100 = A Account
   b. 60–79 = B Account
   c. 40–59 = C Account
   d. Below 40 = D/No-Touch Account

   There's no universally correct formula. Start simple and refine as you test. Watch for clustering. If most accounts land in B, revisit your trait scoring to improve spread and discrimination.

4. **Implement in CRM or Spreadsheet**
   Build the scoring logic into your CRM using formula fields, enrichment data, or built-in AI tools. If you're not ready for CRM automation, use a spreadsheet as a temporary solution to score a list of accounts. Ensure the model is documented and accessible for testing and iteration.

FIGURE 16: Account Scoring Example

Max Score	Trait	Selections	Selection Scores
30	Employee Count	1-50	0
		51-200	15
		201-500	30
		501-1000	30
		1000+	0
20	Industry	Fashion and Apparel	20
		Home and Decor	20
		Sports and Outdoor	10
		Electronics Retail	10
		Health and Beauty	5
10	Region	NAM	10
		EMEA	10
		APAC	5
		ROW	0

5. **Test and Validate**
   Run the model against a sample of known accounts—ideally recent wins, expansions, and losses. Ask Sales, Marketing, and Customer Success leaders to review the assigned scores and validate whether they align with real-world account quality.
6. **Train Teams and Launch**
   Host a training session with Reps and Marketing. Walk through the logic, explain how it works, and how it will automate account selection for the Reps. Both teams need to trust the scoring logic for it to become embedded in daily workflows.

As RevOps works on account scoring, your marketing leader should begin Step 6 in parallel. This builds on your ICP by identifying the key people in those top ICP accounts to target and crafting the messaging that will resonate with them.

STEP 6: PERSONAS AND POSITIONING

Owner: *Marketing Leader,* **Duration:** *14 Days (Days 52–66)*

Personas are practical archetypes of your ideal buyers based on their role on the buying committee (e.g., champion, user, decision maker). Personas humanize the buyer for your go-to-market teams, which in turn guides them, as customer-facing teams, to better target and engage those buyers in a personalized way.

Personas differ from the Ideal Customer Profile in that they are specific to the buyer whereas an ICP is specific to the account. For example, if you wanted to target the director of HR at a $15M healthcare company. You would use the Ideal Customer Profile to first identify the $15M healthcare accounts you want to break into and then the persona to better understand how to target and message the director of HR at those accounts.

Positioning statements complement personas and equip your team with tailored lower-funnel *Why us?* messaging meant to address the unique needs for each type of buyer. Positioning statements answer the question *Why should I choose your solution over competitors or over status quo?* A good positioning statement includes a concise value proposition (the problem you solve and why change is needed), a key differentiator (what makes you different), and a proof point to back up your claim.

Positioning Example:

Our performance management platform helps HR leaders eliminate manual performance review processes and drive manager adoption. Unlike complex HR suites, we integrate seamlessly with your existing HRIS tools, ensuring compliance and no disruption to your workflows. Customers see a 2x increase in manager participation in the first review cycle.

BUILD AN AI PERSONA AGENT

Instead of starting from scratch each time, Marketing, Sales, and Customer Success teams can use AI to generate tailored copy, messaging frameworks, or call guides, all grounded in the same ICP and persona intel.

How to Build the Persona Messaging Agent

- Upload ICP tiers from Chapter 4 into AI tool of your choice.
- Define the messaging framework criteria. Note the brand tone, value propositions, and campaign themes.
- Build a structured prompt that includes:
    - persona context, content type (e.g., email, ad, script, etc.)
    - tone and style guardrails
    - messaging focus (e.g., urgency, ROI, simplicity)
    - campaign theme
- Train the AI agent with a few high-quality messaging examples in different formats; note what you like and don't like.
- Deploy as a Custom GPT or Internal AI Agent.

Reusable GPT Prompt Example (Base Layer)

You are a B2B SaaS copywriter. You are writing [*type of content*] for a [*job title*] at a [*company profile*] who is considering solutions in [*category*]. This persona is responsible for [*key responsibilities*] and is currently facing [*primary pain points*].

Our product is differentiated by [*key differentiators*] and has proven results such as [*proof points*]. Objections you may encounter include [*common objections*], which we overcome by [*response strategies*].

Use a [*tone & style*] that aligns with the way this persona thinks and communicates. Avoid [*style guardrails*]. Prioritize [*desired messaging focus, e.g., clarity, urgency, ROI*].

CEO TL;DR

Personas and Positioning Implementation Steps

1. **Create Personas:** Identify key buyer roles (champion, decision-maker, and user) and develop profiles, including job title, goals, challenges, and buying triggers.
2. **Add Positioning:** Build positioning statements that include value proposition, differentiators, and proof points personalized to each persona.
3. **Validate:** Conduct customer interviews to validate the persona profiles and A/B test positioning statements in Rep and Marketing emails for sanity check.
4. **Train Teams:** Ensure Sales, Marketing, and Customer Success teams know how to use personas and positioning in their workflows.

How to Create Personas and Positioning (for Your Team)

At a minimum, expect your Marketing team to follow the steps below for effective personas and positioning. If any of these elements are missing, the work may not be ready for rollout.

1. **Create Buyer Personas**
   Start by identifying which buyer roles warrant distinct personas. A persona may differ based on role (e.g., champion vs. decision-maker) or by segment (e.g., SMB vs. Mid-Market champions often have different needs, goals, and constraints). For each persona, build a profile that includes:
   a. Job Title
   b. Buying Role
   c. Key Responsibilities
   d. Positioning Statement
   e. Need or Pain
   f. Benefits from Using our Product
   g. Common Objections & How to Handle Them
   h. GPT Instructions
2. **Validate with Research**
   Avoid relying solely on internal assumptions. Personas should reflect how buyers actually behave, not just how we assume they do.
   a. Aim to interview at least two current and two churned customers for each persona.
   b. Add input from customer-facing teams in Product, Customer Success, and Sales.
   c. Leverage call-listening tools or AI features in your CRM and MAP to help surface objections and themes.
3. **Add Positioning Statements**
   Develop one positioning statement per persona. Each statement should clearly articulate:
   a. **The Value Proposition:** What problem you solve and why they need to make a change now (with urgency).
   b. **The Differentiator:** Why your solution is a better fit for

them than competitors or than sticking with the status quo (e.g., manual workarounds, no solution in place).

c. **Proof Points:** One to three data points or case studies that validate your claims.

Expect value propositions to vary slightly based on the ICP segment or persona. Below are two examples of positioning statements for an HR platform tailored to different personas: one for small-business owners and one for mid-market businesses. Each reflects the same product but highlights different value propositions, differentiators, and proof points based on the buyer's unique needs.

Positioning Example #1: *HR Director in the Mid-Market Segment (Company size 200–1,000 employees)*

↳ For HR directors scaling fast without the admin headcount to match, our performance platform replaces manual feedback loops and inconsistent reviews with a simple system for structured goals, real-time feedback, and manager accountability. Built for lean teams, it integrates easily with your existing HRIS, so there's no heavy lift; just faster cycles and better visibility.

↳ Customers spend 50% less time on managing performance cycles and experience a 3x increase in manager participation in the first two quarters.

Positioning Example #2: *HR Director in the Enterprise Segment (Company size 1,000+ employees)*

↳ For HR directors at large enterprises managing distributed teams and complex org structures, our platform brings performance under one roof, standardizing goal-setting, feedback, and reviews among different business units without sacrificing flexibility. Unlike legacy HCM suites, we enable cross-functional visibility and high adoption without IT bottlenecks.

↳ 90% of global teams achieve full rollout within 60 days. Customers see a 4x improvement in feedback completion rates throughout departments.

4. **Validate with Stakeholders**
   Review persona and positioning drafts with Sales, Product, and Customer Success leaders to capture objections, reactions, and feedback.

5. **Train Teams**
   Train Sales and Customer Success teams about how and when to use the personas, GPT instructions, and positioning. Make personas, positioning statements, and GPT instructions available to Reps to reinforce adoption.

With execution underway, your next move as CEO is to ensure the ICP definition is translating into measurable outcomes. The next chapter walks through how to assess progress, spot early red flags, and report performance back to the board.

HR Director for Small Business

Job Title: HR Director
Buying Role: Decision-Maker

KEY RESPONSIBILITIES

- Manage performance review process.
- Improve employee engagement and retention.
- Equip managers with tools for feedback and development.
- Standardize HR systems and reduce manual HR work.

POSITIONING STATEMENT

Our performance management platform helps HR leaders move from manual, inconsistent review processes to structured systems that managers actually use. Unlike heavy HCM suites, we're purpose-built for lean teams; quick to roll out, easy to adopt, and simple to maintain. Most customers with fewer than 500 employees see a 3x increase in manager participation and cut review cycle time by 50%.

NEED OR PAIN

Manual reviews are time-consuming, inconsistent, and poorly adopted by managers. The process feels like a compliance task rather than a driver of performance.

BENEFITS FROM USING OUR PRODUCT

- Saves time through automation and templates.
- Improves manager participation.
- Delivers better visibility into team performance.

COMMON OBJECTIONS & HANDLING

- ***"We're too small to switch systems."***
  "That's why we designed it for speed: live in days, not months."
- ***"Our managers won't use it."***
  "It's built for them with lightweight UX, no training required."
- ***"We just changed our process."***
  "We integrate into what's working; no need to start over."

FOR GPT

- **Competitive Insight:** Differentiate on speed to implement; ease of use for managers; purpose-built for SMBs.
- **Tone & Style:** Use plainspoken, professional, outcomes-oriented tone.
- **Content Guardrails:** Avoid vague claims and jargon. Prioritize clarity, specificity, and persona fit.

FIGURE 17: Buyer Persona Template

Name:	
Job Title(s):	Buying Role:
Key Responsibilities:	Need or Pain:
Benefits From Using Our Product:	Positioning Statement:
Elevator Pitch:	GPT Instructions:
Common Objections:	Objection Handling/Taking Points:

EXECUTIVE SUMMARY 6

HOW CEOS MEASURE THE ICP DECISION

Key Takeaways

- **ICP Isn't a One-Time Exercise**
  It requires active monitoring and realignment as growth goals and market dynamics evolve.
- **ICP Affects Commercial Efficiency Metrics**
  As an indicator of market fit, ICP affects outcomes like ARR value, new bookings, logos won, and churn. These metrics indicate whether you're winning the right customers.
- **In Defining Your ICP, You Set Your Company Benchmarks**
  The win rate, sales cycle time, churn rate, and deal size data points that define your ICP in turn also serve as your company benchmarks.
- **Diagnosing ICP Issues is Diagnosing Market Fit**
  In isolation, ICP issues can point to execution gaps, but when they are seen in combination, they can indicate deeper issues related to market fit.

ICP Measurement Deliverables

By the end of this chapter, you should have:

- Internal Reporting on ICP Performance
- Board Reporting on ICP Impact
- ICP Red Flags Diagnostic

Why Measuring the ICP Matters

Executing on the ICP Decision is how CEOs connect growth assumptions with real-world implementation. Measuring the impact of that execution proves that your company can win reliably and efficiently.

When CEOs track ICP health using both internal execution metrics and board-facing commercial outcomes, they build the next layer of predictability into their growth plans. A well-embedded ICP shows up in the leading indicators of scalable growth: shorter sales cycles, higher close rates, better retention, and healthier unit economics.

If the ICP is not a fit, no amount of sales effort or marketing spend will deliver the outcomes your board is expecting. CEOs who react to early warning signs, like low conversion rates and rising churn from their core customer segments, can adjust before it becomes more than just a missed quarter.

6

HOW CEOS MEASURE THE ICP DECISION

THE ICP DEFINITION isn't static: It evolves as growth targets or market conditions change. This chapter helps you identify the health of your ICP definition, whether it's time to revisit the definition or adjust execution and how to report on it back to the board.

INTERNAL REPORTING: IS YOUR ICP WORKING?

Once your team begins embedding your ICP definition, the goal is traction. This section outlines a short list of metrics you can use with your go-to-market leaders to track progress to results. ICP tracking does require that your CRM supports ICP tiers and consistently tags accounts accordingly.

Weekly (Execution Check):

- **Logos Won by ICP Tier:** Are we closing deals in the right segments?
- **Opportunities by ICP Tier:** Is the pipeline filling with high-fit accounts?

Monthly (Performance Check):

- **Median Deal Size for A/B Accounts:** Are we winning the right-sized customers?
- **Sales Cycle for A/B Accounts:** Are deals moving faster where fit is strongest?

While these internal metrics help you manage execution, the board is looking for evidence that your ICP definition is translating into growth. The next set of metrics demonstrates how these internal efforts show up as commercial outcomes.

BOARD REPORTING: HOW ICP AFFECTS COMMERCIAL OUTCOMES

Each of the four growth decisions affects the common commercial metrics many boards track, but certain decisions influence specific board metrics more directly than others.

For ICP, the most immediate impact is on market expansion and early indicators of customer fit, reflected in outcomes like ARR value, new bookings, logos won, and churn. These metrics indicate whether you're winning the right customers and establishing a foundation for scalable growth.

In later chapters, we'll explore how the SLA and Contribution Decisions build on your ICP and shape pipeline creation, lead quality, and sales execution. The metrics in Figure 18 are the ones most likely to shift when the ICP Decision is executed well. The others, shaded in gray, will be explored in later chapters as we unpack the remaining CEO decisions.

RED FLAGS: WHEN TO REVISIT THE ICP

ICP red flags point to an issue with market fit. Market fit issues can look like declining lead volume on the same spend from Marketing, Reps chasing and not landing bigger accounts, relying heavily on discounting, or deals lost on features or to competition. In isolation, each of these anecdotes can point to execution gaps, but when they are seen in combination, they can indicate deeper issues related to ICP. Once you've ruled out poor execution, it's time

FIGURE 18: Commercial Board Metrics Tied to ICP

Board Metric	Formula	Most Influenced By
ARR Value	Sum of all contracted recurring revenue × 12 months	ICP
New Business Bookings	Total $ of Closed-Won Deals (New Logos Only)	ICP
Logos Won	# of New Logos in Period	ICP
Close Rate	Closed-Won Deals ÷ SQLs	ICP
Deal Size	(Average) Total Closed-Won Revenue ÷ # of Closed-Won Deals or (Median) Middle Value	ICP
Churn Rate	Lost Customers ÷ Total Customers (Start of Period)	ICP
Sales Cycle (Days)	Avg # of Days from First Contact to Close	SLA
Lead-to-Opp Rate	# of Opportunities Created ÷ # of Leads Accepted (SALs) or # of Leads Qualified (MQLs)	SLA
Pipeline Value ($)	Sum of Open Pipeline	Contribution
Pipeline Coverage Ratio (0.0)	Total Pipeline for the Period ÷ Quota for the Period	Contribution
Opportunities Created	# of SQLs or SAOs Created in Period	Contribution

to revisit whether you're still focused on the right target.

Metrics Red Flags (when seen in combination)

- Healthy marketing spend, but declining leads or opportunities
- Lower than expected deal size
- Closed-lost reasons related to features or competition
- Rising churn rate or falling NPS scores
- Churn reasons indicating lack of value, low adoption, or missing features

Market Dynamics Flags

- Shifts in competitive landscape (e.g., commoditized features, new entrants)

- Changes in customer behavior or needs
- Slowing new logo growth in top A segments

In the event market dynamics shift, teams need to adapt by proactively reevaluating the ICP segments. Without reassessing the ICP, Marketing may continue to spend on prospects who are not sales-ready, driving up CAC, and Sales may struggle to convert leads into opportunities, driving down revenue. If teams don't stop to reassess the market at this point, they waste time on budget-chasing tactics that no longer match the reality of the market.

Now that you've defined your ICP, executed against it, and established a way to track its performance, it's time to shift from who you're targeting to how your teams work together to convert those targets into qualified pipeline.

CASE STUDY

Bigger Isn't Always Better

The CFO of a $28M hospitality technology company forecasted ARR targets for the first year of the investment based on the expected average deal size, not realizing that the average deal size number was skewed by two unusually large deals. By using the average in the model without sanity-checking it first, the CFO had inadvertently set up the commercial teams to chase larger than usual accounts. As a result, Sales began chasing leads that looked "enterprise" on paper, and Marketing shifted campaign targeting to meet the demand for larger accounts opportunities. Everyone assumed bigger deals would drive faster growth.

Instead, the opposite happened. Growth declined. The platform was built for speed and simplicity; it wasn't designed to meet the complex needs of enterprise buyers. As opportunities stalled in the pipeline, Marketing pulled spend forward to fill more at the top of the funnel. Sales messaged the stall in pipeline as a result of the longer sales cycle common with enterprise accounts. Although the Reps struggled to close the larger accounts at scale, they continued to prioritize working them over "smaller" deals. Come board time, the CEO was left to trying to explain the miss on bookings when execution and process hadn't changed.

WHAT THE CEO HEARD FROM THE TEAM

- "We're getting into big accounts, but they take longer to close."
- "These buyers are asking for integrations we don't have."
- "We're losing more deals than we used to, and the ones we win aren't renewing."

WHAT THE CEO SAW IN THE DATA

- Low lead-to-opportunity conversion
- Declining close rates
- Increasing "closed-lost" reasons tied to product gaps and feature comparisons

SOLUTION

The CEO knew something was amiss but couldn't put their finger on what exactly the problem was. They decided to start at the beginning by assessing account fit with the ICP Workshop. In the roundtable discussion with the team, they quickly uncovered a key misalignment: The commercial teams had shifted their focus to enterprise accounts without first validating whether those buyers were a fit for the product at scale. Sales and Marketing had internalized the CFO's forecast assumptions, chasing logos that didn't align with the product's roadmap or strengths.

To course-correct, the RevOps leader underwent a segmentation analysis to validate the ICP and gut-check the benchmarks associated with their best customers. As expected, the team found that accounts with more than 5k employee had longer sales cycles and far worse close rates than accounts with 500–2k employees. The SMB and Mid-Market (MM) accounts converted faster, retained longer, and required fewer customizations.

Confident in their insights, the leadership team re-oriented on the SMB and MM ICP segments. They re-tiered target accounts in the CRM to reinforce the importance of selling to companies of the correct size, right-sized campaign tactics to reach the buyers, and re-forecasted the bottom-up Contribution Model (Part III) to set lead and opportunity targets that aligned better with a more realistic selling price. It took one quarter for pipeline coverage to rebound and two quarters to see close rate, and bookings, return to health.

PART II

THE SLA DECISION

EXECUTIVE SUMMARY

THE SLA DECISION DEFINED

Key Takeaways

- **Forecast Accuracy Depends on the SLA**
  A strong SLA defines the lead progression and attribution process that all commercial teams use to convert leads to pipeline. This shared process makes pipeline tracking, forecast accuracy, and sourced bookings accountability possible.
- **The Push SLA Is Different**
  This SLA is more than just an agreement between two teams. It architects how your CRM and MAP are built to enforce lead quality, attribution, and accountability for lead conversion at scale.
- **Sharing One Process is the Best Practice**
  An SLA for new business only works when both sales and marketing leaders co-own the design. This collaboration ensures buy-in, alignment, and shared accountability for pipeline outcomes.
- **SLA Protects Profitability**
  Increasing spend in pipeline sources like inbound, outbound, or partners without an SLA in place risks wasted dollars as you operate without a system to turn leads to pipeline.
- **The SLA Is a Prerequisite for the Contribution Decision (Part III)**
  You can't reliably assign budget, headcount, or pipeline targets until teams agree on lead stages, qualification criteria, and handoff timing.

Why the SLA Decision Matters

A well-built SLA protects LTV:CAC and improves forecast accuracy. It gives CEOs the data clarity they need to allocate spend, track ROI, and drive profitable growth. Without a defined and enforced SLA, your GTM teams operate on assumptions, Reps cherry-pick leads, and Marketing can't optimize spend reliably. In extreme cases, morale between teams erodes as trust deteriorates across teams and CEOs are left wondering where to invest for scale or what to fix in the event of a decline.

The Push SLA changes that. It creates a single, shared process for how to turn leads to pipeline, co-owned by Sales, Marketing, BDRs, and RevOps. The Push SLA goes further than typical SLAs by expanding the standard timing SLA to include team decisions about lead scoring, attribution, and email compliance. Those decisions then become the systems requirements for your CRM and MAP. This is how you your CRM into a single source of truth for all commercial reporting.

7

THE SERVICE-LEVEL AGREEMENT (SLA) DECISION DEFINED

GENERALLY SPEAKING, the Service-Level Agreement (SLA) Decision establishes the rules of engagement for how your teams manage, qualify, and move leads through the funnel. As it relates to new business sales, the SLA sets the process behind which Marketing, BDRs, and Sales convert leads to pipeline. This chapter walks you through what a strong SLA looks like for *new deals* and why it matters.

Allow about 33 days from kick-off to launch for the SLA Decision to be made and executed. If you are following the 100-Day Plan schedule, this marks Days 67–100. The Push SLA steps include:

- 2 days for the SLA Workshop (see Chapter 8, Step 7)
- 30 days for system configuration and QA
- 1 day for Rep training and certification

The Push SLA sets the foundation for reliable forecasting and predictable pipeline conversion. When operationalized, it protects profitability among different pipeline sources, whether they be inbound, outbound, or partner, by ensuring that sourced leads are acted on with urgency and not wasted. An SLA gives CEOs some confidence that an increased investment in these lead sources is more likely to result in qualified pipeline and, ultimately, revenue.

The Push SLA answers the question of *What will we do with a lead when we get one?* It defines how leads move through the funnel: who owns them, what qualifies them, and how they're tracked. Without a clearly defined SLA process in place, your teams can't reliably forecast performance, react to conversion issues, or optimize ROI by channel.

SLAs commonly refer to the handoff between Marketing and Sales as it relates to inbound sales, but they can be established between any teams coordinating efforts to achieve an outcome. Other commercial SLA examples include:

- **Product and Sales** (e.g., self-serve, free trial/freemium conversion)
- **Customer Success and Sales** (e.g., cross-sell or expansion sales)
- **BDRs and Account Executives** (e.g., outbound sales motion)

This book focuses on the *inbound* sales use case, where an SLA is established between Marketing, BDRs, and Sales to define the qualification process for marketing-sourced leads. If these teams can organize behind a shared SLA, then it's generally easy to retrofit that SLA to accommodate other selling motions. Whenever different teams share responsibility for pipeline creation, you'll need them to also share a well-defined SLA to mitigate the risk of lead leakage inherent with one or more handoffs.

In *The Push Framework*, the SLA Decision is more than just a simple definition of who owns the lead at different stages. It is a structured workshop where Sales, Marketing, and RevOps collaborate to define lead stages, qualification criteria, timing expectations, attribution rules, and a regulation-compliant email process. It touches on all the critical upper funnel alignment points shared between Sales, BDRs and Marketing.

WHAT MAKES THE PUSH SLA DIFFERENT?

Some companies treat the SLA as a basic agreement on lead follow-up timing between Marketing and Sales, but this kind of lightweight SLA rarely holds up under pressure. When the SLA only addresses alignment related to timing follow-up, it often lacks system reinforcement and shared ownership, making it easy to ignore and hard to govern.

The Push SLA Framework is different. It goes beyond timing agreements to also include the system and process architecture that turns leads into pipeline. The Push SLA Workshop walks teams through a deliberate series of decision-making sessions that align the different teams around a singular process for qualifying, tracking, and progressing incoming leads. The decisions made in this workshop are captured in a way to become build requirements for both your CRM and MAP. Doing so ensures systems support your process rather than the other way around.

Here's what sets the Push SLA apart:

- **Built by All Those Who Work the Funnel**
  The Push Framework brings together the leaders and operators who run the funnel every day (Sales, Marketing, RevOps, BDRs, and Demand Gen) and guides them through making the key alignment decisions that will power lead progression. Together, they define qualification stages, follow-up timing, handoff rules, and exit criteria. The result is a system your team believes in because they helped build it.
- **Turns Your CRM into a Single Source of Truth for Reporting**
  The Push SLA isn't a static document. It is the architecture behind how your CRM and MAP are configured. It informs the build of lifecycle stages, lead scoring, qualification criteria, attribution tracking, and email compliance. This ensures your systems reinforce the agreed-upon processes. While the setup can be rigorous, it is this architecture that enables your CRM to become a trusted "source of truth" reporting system for both Sales and Marketing.

- **Protects LTV:CAC and Bookings Accountability**
  Most SLAs stop at lead handoff rules. Because *The Push Framework* goes further into attribution set-up, it enables CEOs to assign bookings targets to teams other than Sales, like Marketing, Partner, Product, and Customer Success. It gives you the infrastructure to track and measure ROI by channel, hold teams accountable, and protect LTV:CAC.

WHY THE SLA DECISION COMES SECOND

Once you have made the ICP decision and your team understands which segments to target, the next step is to define how those targets will convert into customers. If you're following the 100-Day Plan schedule, you'll first define your ICP to select which sales motions and which pipeline sources to activate. These inputs help you understand what types of SLA to implement.

Like the ICP Decision, the SLA Decision can happen anytime during the hold period. Tell-tale signs that it's time to revisit the SLA sound like "We have a strong close rate, we just need more leads!" (from Sales) or "We're sending leads, but Sales is cherry-picking which ones to work!" (from Marketing). When these sound bites are coupled with a lower-than-expected lead-to-opportunity rate, it's a sign to revisit the SLA. Because the SLA Decision can be a net-new process, with no pre-requisites, teams often see improvements in lead-to-opportunity conversion rates and increased pipeline coverage relatively soon after Reps are trained.

The SLA Decision is also a critical prerequisite to Contribution Modeling (see Part III): the process of assigning pipeline and bookings targets to different sources like Marketing for inbound sales, BDRs for outbound, Product or Marketing for self-serve, and Partners for indirect sales. While the SLA doesn't have to be fully implemented before setting contribution goals, key SLA Decisions that come out of the workshop on funnel stage naming and timing must be agreed upon. These shared stages are what you'll set goals against in the upcoming Contribution Decision.

ROLE OF THE CEO

The SLA presents a unique challenge for commercial teams. The marketing leader's success depends on executing the SLA properly, yet the responsibility for execution primarily falls to BDR and sales leaders. Your role is simply to ensure that all teams follow through with the SLA.

It would be a mistake to view the SLA as merely a process coordination effort between these teams. Once implemented, the Push SLA establishes the configuration of your company's commercial data infrastructure. This foundation allows your team to diagnose funnel conversions, track pipeline, and optimize ROI. It sets up the reporting system you'll use to demonstrate profitable growth to your investors and future buyers.

As CEO, your role is one of oversight: ensuring alignment, urgency, and proper resource allocation are in place so teams have what they need to complete execution quickly and correctly.

1. **Champion Accountability & Urgency:** The SLA Decision informs the reporting infrastructure for your Sales and Marketing teams. Without it, they cannot build or ensure a predictable revenue engine. Regularly check in with sales and marketing leaders to ensure strong buy-in and mutual involvement throughout the decision and execution phases.
2. **Secure Resources:** Because this is an alignment exercise, the heads of both Sales and Marketing should be in seat before you begin. The company should also have a CRM onboarded and, at minimum, a MAP identified, if not onboarded. Since the SLA Decision will shape their configuration, these systems do not have to be fully optimized before starting.

COMMON CEO MISTAKE: INCREASING MARKETING SPEND WITHOUT AN SLA

Many CEOs mistakenly assume that more marketing spend will simply equate to more pipeline, but without a clearly defined SLA in place that's implemented in systems and enforced by sales managers, those leads (and dollars) can easily leak out of the funnel and go to waste.

Without an SLA in place:

- Reps might cherry-pick or ignore leads.
- Attribution may be unreliable.
- Marketing may be unable to deliver efficient leads at lower costs.

Each of these creates a hole in your funnel, which is why you wait to invest in marketing programs until your SLA is in place. Instead, build the SLA architecture (stages, rules, system configurations) before you increase lead volume. Otherwise, you may be pouring leads into a leaky funnel with no way to trace what worked, what didn't, or what ROI to expect.

WHEN TO OUTSOURCE

If you have an internal team capable of building the SLA Decision into your CRM and MAP systems, outsourcing may not be necessary. However, if you lack in-house expertise to build, it's worth investing in a third party to ensure the system is built quickly and correctly the first time.

While it's recommended to outsource the system build if needed, do not outsource the decision-making in its entirety without your sales and marketing leaders involved to guide the process. When this system is built without your leaders' involvement, you may see adoption fail or miss the mark. In these cases, the team can find itself back at square one, needing to revisit SLA Decisions long after the third-party engagement ends, which can set you back months. Avoid this by ensuring sales and marketing leadership drive the decision-making process.

That said, there is value in outsourcing facilitation. The Push SLA Workshop covers a number of shared decisions between multiple teams. If your team needs a guide to navigate it all or if alignment between Sales and Marketing has historically been tense, consider bringing in an experienced outside facilitator to run the workshop. A facilitator will be seen as objective and can guide the discussion, pressure-test assumptions, and ensure the final playbook reflects a realistic shared system design.

Now that you understand what a strong SLA looks like and why it matters, the next chapter will show you how to lead your team through the five key alignment decisions that connect Sales and Marketing into a single, coordinated commercial unit.

CASE STUDY

"We Need More Leads"

The CEO of a $25M cybersecurity company had increased the marketing budget after closing on their new round of funding, but those new leads were not turning into opportunities as expected. Pipeline began to suffer, and the company missed its bookings target in the first quarter of its new investment. Sales claimed the close rate was strong and if they just had more good leads, they could make up for the bookings gap. Marketing said they were sending more leads, but Sales was cherry-picking who to contact and not following up quickly enough. Sales was resolute that more leads would result in more deals, but more leads required even more budget, and the CEO was concerned with how inefficiency would affect margin. This situation caused a rift between the Sales and Marketing teams, bringing down morale on both sides and leading to finger-pointing. The CEO felt stuck trying to resolve this dispute without clear data or a way forward.

WHAT THE CEO HEARD FROM THE TEAM

- "We need more leads."
- "MQLs are 'bad quality.'"
- "Sales isn't working the leads we send them."

WHAT THE CEO SAW IN THE DATA

- Lead-to-Meeting Booked Rate declined
- Days in working status longer than expected
- LTV:CAC declined

SOLUTION

Misalignment on lead qualification was wasting marketing dollars. Leads were going stale without timely Sales follow-up, and Marketing lacked the feedback loop needed to optimize the campaign. The CEO paused the planned budget increase and directed the heads of Sales and Marketing to work through the SLA Workshop and align on qualification criteria, timing, and handoff rules. The budget pause created urgency. Once the SLA was implemented in the CRM and MAP, and the Reps were certified on the process through training, Marketing was able to increase spend, deliver more leads, and most importantly, make adjustments to spend based on lead quality reporting fed back from Sales. As a result of the shared process, pipeline coverage began to improve in the quarter after launch.

EXECUTIVE SUMMARY 8

HOW CEOS MAKE THE SLA DECISION

Key Takeaways

1. **The Push SLA Workshop Architects Your GTM Engine**
   This one- or two-day workshop sequences the five shared decisions your cross-functional team must agree on to quickly turn your CRM into a reliable source of truth for reporting.
2. **You Are Codifying Your Revenue Operations Playbook.**
   The workshop outputs become your GTM infrastructure guide, used to build systems, train reps, and onboard new team members.
3. **Your Role is Not to Design the Process**
   Nominate sales and marketing leaders to own the workshop and lead the sessions. Your job is to unblock, align, and ensure decisions are made with urgency and shared among the teams.
4. **RevOps and Training Need to Be in the Room**
   An SLA that can't be built or trained won't work. If you haven't identified a sales trainer or the person who will build your systems, then assign or outsource one before the workshop. They will need to participate fully in the workshop for this to work.

Chapter 8 Deliverables

After running the Push SLA Workshop, your company will have:

- Documented Lead Stages and Exit Criteria
- Lead Quality Defined
- Codified SLA Rules of Engagement
- Lead Scoring Logic Established
- Attribution Rules Defined
- Centralized Email Process Established
- Revenue Operations Playbook Finalized

Why Making the SLA Decision Matters

The Push SLA Workshop aligns Sales, Marketing, and RevOps on the five key components that drive pipeline conversion: lead stages, qualification criteria and timing, lead scoring logic, attribution rules, and compliant email governance. These are the decisions that define how your funnel actually works: who owns what, when, and how.

When these elements are treated in silos, GTM execution breaks down. Sales wastes time on leads that aren't sales-ready, Marketing gets blamed for poor pipeline, and the CEO is left with an inability to understand breakdowns or direct resources efficiently.

This chapter gives your team the structure to make these decisions quickly and collaboratively, resulting in a *Revenue Operations Playbook* that becomes the build specs for your CRM and MAP systems and the training framework for your codified lead to pipeline conversion process.

For CEOs, the Push SLA Workshop is a forcing function for creating cross-functional accountability and a shared commitment to lead-to-pipeline conversion performance. These decisions lay the groundwork for scalable, measurable growth and must be in place before you and the CFO can forecast accurately.

8

HOW CEOS MAKE THE SLA DECISION

DURATION: 2 DAYS FOR DECISION (DAYS 67–68)

THE SLA establishes the critical coordination decisions between Sales and Marketing, shaping how leads progress through the funnel and how revenue attribution is measured. These decisions directly inform the CRM architecture, transforming it into a shared data warehouse for Sales, Marketing and Revenue Operations.

Without a codified SLA, Sales and Marketing operate in silos. When this disconnection slows down pipeline, it can cause friction between the teams as "lead quality" or "lead follow-up" get called into question. A well-structured SLA assigns the roles, funnel stages, timing, and qualification criteria for each handoff point within the funnel so that teams can operate with a shared responsibility for lead progression. For CEOs, defining an SLA using *The Push Framework* is the mechanism that transforms a CRM into a single source of truth for commercial reporting.

This chapter introduces the Push SLA Workshop, a cross-functional series of working sessions designed to guide Sales, Marketing, and RevOps through the five shared decisions required to convert leads to pipeline *reliably*. These five decisions are made during a one- or two-day workshop (in-person) or up to a week of virtual working sessions.

The five alignment decisions covered in the Push SLA Workshop are:

- Lead Qualification Stages and Roles
- SLA on Timing and Qualification Criteria
- Lead Score Logic to Back into Qualification Criteria
- Attribution Reporting Rules of Engagement
- Centralized Email Process Between Sales and Marketing

Condensing these five decisions into a one- or two-day alignment workshop is a powerful way to unite the teams under a singular process and gain early traction on adoption. The structure defined here assumes a two-day in-person workshop to cover all five decisions as a group. However, this agenda can flex: It can be condensed to fill one-day or be extended from two days in person to up to one week virtually. Avoid letting the sessions extend beyond a week. By keeping the workshop sessions to fewer than five days, you drive the urgency needed to help teams connect the dots between the decisions they are making from one session to the next. For your teams, understanding how these decisions all connect is a critical part of the learning baked into the Push SLA agenda.

If you can, it's best to host the SLA Workshop in person. While these decision sessions can be done virtually over the course of several days, the cultural benefits of doing this in person in one or two days often outweigh the convenience of virtual sessions. When facilitated live, the SLA Workshop can mark a transformational milestone as Sales and Marketing bond over creating a shared process in the same room, in real time, in one go.

THE PUSH SLA WORKSHOP AGENDA

The Push SLA Workshop is comprised of five sessions during which the Sales and Marketing team codify the company's *Revenue Operations Playbook*. This playbook includes the key decisions made cross-functionally by the team in these sessions and will be used by RevOps or the third-party build partner as the architecture to build or update the CRM and MAP platforms later in the execution phase (see Chapter 9). The five alignment sessions are the following:

Session #1: Define the Lead Qualification Stages

Sounds simple, but you'd be surprised how deep misalignment about stage names, owners, and actions can be. This first session establishes the naming, definitions, and ownership of the lead qualification stages that occur between lead capture and pipeline creation. Your team must align to these stage definitions first before they can define the process, timing, and qualification criteria for moving prospects through them in the SLA session that follows.

Session #2: Codify the SLA

In this session, the team walks through each lead stage defined in Session #1 to establish its rules of engagement. You'll decide how long a lead can remain in each stage before being rejected or recycled, what outreach activities are required from the Rep, and which disqualification or closed-lost reasons should be available in the CRM.

The team will also define the minimum qualification criteria a prospect must meet to book an initial sales meeting with a sales rep (e.g., to convert to SQL) and, later, to open pipeline (e.g., convert to SQO). These decisions will directly inform the lead-scoring logic built in Session #3.

Session #3: Map Lead Score

This session can be limited to a smaller working group (typically the RevOps lead, BDR lead, and Demand Generation lead). Using the qualification criteria established in Session #2, the team defines the lead-scoring logic that the MAP will use to act as an early filter. The goal is to prioritize leads that meet your minimum criteria for a Sales meeting, enabling Reps to focus their time on the highest-fit prospects.

Session #4: Set Attribution Rules of Engagement

The fourth session can be limited to the RevOps lead, Sales, and leaders who oversee the different lead sources (e.g., paid search, events, etc.). This session standardizes the naming convention that will be used in the CRM to track attribution and dictates the rules for how, so the teams can select a channel or lead source to attribute. The session also guides the team to decide which additional attribution data has to be collected for fulsome ROI reporting.

Session #5: Centralize the Email Process

The final session guides the team to define a compliant opt-in/opt-out process that can be used across Marketing, Sales, and Customer Success. The group aligns on which opt-in/opt-out fields to include in the CRM and MAP, sets the rules for suppression files, and identifies the owner responsible for managing the email channel among the different functions.

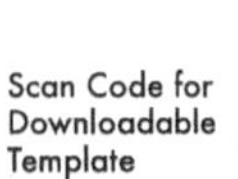

FIGURE 19: Two-Day Push SLA Workshop Agenda

Day	Duration	Agenda	Owner	Attendees
1	2 Hours	**Session #1: Define the Lead Qualification Stages** *(Must be defined before moving on to any of the following sessions)*	Sales or Marketing Leader	• Head of Sales • Head of Marketing • Demand Generation Lead • Head of BDRs • RevOps Lead • Sales Trainer
	4 Hours	**Session #2: Codify the SLA**	Sales or Marketing Leader	• Head of Sales • Head of Marketing • BDR Manager • 1–2 Sales Reps (reps on the phones) • Demand Generation Lead • RevOps Lead • Sales Trainer
2	1.5 Hours	**Session #3: Map Lead Score**	Marketing Leader	• Head of Marketing • BDR Manager • Demand Generation Lead • RevOps Lead • Sales Trainer
	2 Hours	**Session #4: Set Attribution Rules of Engagement**	RevOps Leader	• Head of Sales • Head of Marketing • BDR Manager • Demand Generation Lead • Partner Lead • RevOps Lead • Sales Trainer
	1 Hour	**Session #5: Centralize the Email Process**	Email Lead	• Head of Sales • Head of Marketing • Head of Customer Success • BDR Manager • Demand Generation Lead • Email Lead • RevOps Lead • Sales Trainer

WORKSHOP OUTPUT: THE REVENUE OPERATIONS PLAYBOOK

The five working sessions address specific points of overlap between the CRM and the MAP. As the team walks through the decisions laid out in the workshop agenda, encourage the team to live-scribe each decision onto a single shared document that can be used later as the build requirements for optimizing your systems. When described in this way, the output of the Push SLA Workshop is documented as your Revenue Operations Playbook, which outlines, in detail, how the teams are expected to progress leads from capture to pipeline and how to build the systems to support that process.

LEAD STAGE DEFINITIONS FOR INBOUND

This chapter walks through how to run the SLA Workshop specific to an *inbound sales motion*. This example includes two handoffs among three teams:

Marketing → BDR → Sales

If your company doesn't use BDRs, you can adjust the framework by assigning qualification responsibilities directly to Account Executives (AE) instead of BDRs and adjusting the handoff logic accordingly. You always want a Rep to own and be accountable for confirming lead quality when booking the first Sales meeting.

The SLA examples in this chapter follow standard inbound lead stages (see Figure 20), defined here as:

- **Lead:** captured via form fill, event, webinar, or another marketing channel.
- **MQL (Marketing-Qualified Lead):** meets lead-scoring threshold in the marketing automation platform (MAP) and routes to a BDR.
- **SQL (Sales-Qualified Lead):** BDR qualifies the lead against minimum criteria and books an initial sales meeting with an AE; no opportunity or pipeline is assigned yet.

- **SAO (Sales-Accepted Opportunity):** AE reviews and accepts the meeting; CRM tracking on opportunity begins, but pipeline remains at $0.
- **SQO (Sales-Qualified Opportunity):** AE holds the first meeting, qualifies the prospect to open pipeline using a sales methodology (e.g., BANT), and schedules the next step with the prospect. Sales owns the deal from here. Pipeline opens, and the inbound SLA is complete.

STANDARDIZE THE FUNNEL AFTER SQL

The early-stage funnel stages may differ depending on the source of the lead. For example, Marketing may deliver "MQLs" from inbound channels, while Partners may deliver "Referrals" from indirect or channel sources (see Figure 21). However, once a Rep qualifies the lead against the minimum criteria to book a meeting and converts it to an SQL, all leads, regardless of source, follow a singular sales funnel with consistent stage names and definitions from Sales Accepted Opportunity (SAO) to closed-lost or won.

In other words, while pre-SQL stages may vary by source, your post-SQL funnel should standardize throughout all motions. The only exception is self-serve or product-led flows, which may follow a separate path.

THE GOAL IS TO QUALIFY THE PROSPECT BEFORE EACH HANDOFF

Our inbound example includes two handoffs among three teams. A successful SLA enables each team to qualify the prospect before handing it off to the next team. In this model, that looks like:

- **MQL as Lead Quality Checkpoint #1**
  Marketing checks quality via lead scoring before handing to a BDR.
- **SQL as Lead Quality Checkpoint #2**
  BDR checks against the minimum qualification criteria to book a meeting before handing to a Rep.

FIGURE 20: Standard Inbound Lead Stages

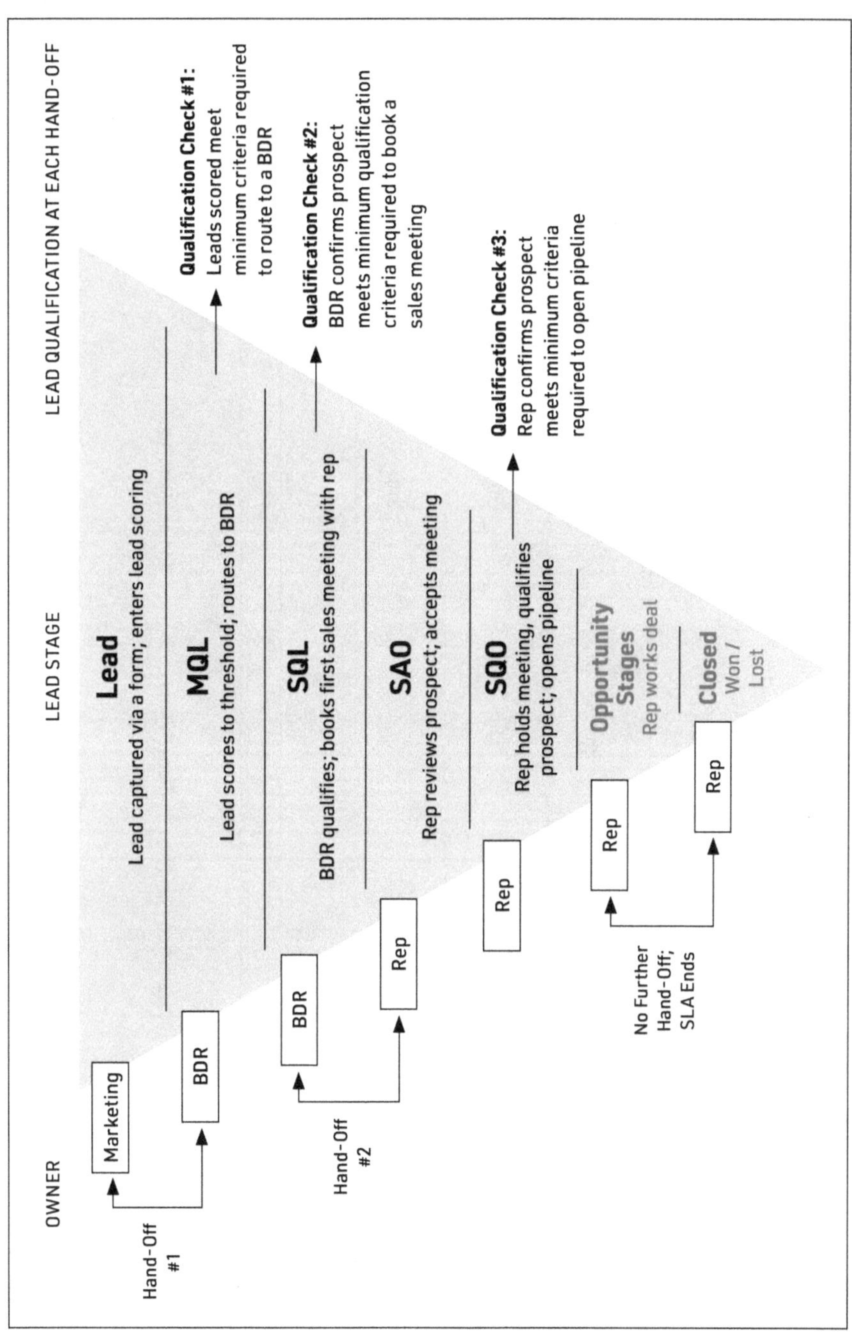

FIGURE 21: Typical Funnel Stages Across Different Selling Motions

Basic Lead Flow	"Inbound" Marketing-Sourced Leads	"Outbound" Direct-Sourced Leads	"Partner" In-Direct-Sourced Leads	"Self-Serve or PLG" Marketing-Sourced Leads
Lead Enters	Lead	Contact	Referral	Site Visitor
Lead Scored (Auto Qualified)	MQL	*Skips this stage*	*Skips this stage*	*Freemium Sign Up*
Meeting Booked (Human Qualified)	SQL	SQL	SQL	Account Activate
Meeting Accepted	SAO	SAO	SAO	Usage
Meeting Held (Opportunity Qualified)	SQO	SQO	SQO	Product-Qualified
Closed Won / Lost	Closed Won / Lost	Closed Won / Lost	Closed Won / Lost	Paid

- **SQO as Lead Quality Checkpoint #3 (Final)**
  Rep checks against minimum qualification criteria to open pipeline before moving to pipeline stages.

Each team involved in a lead handoff must understand how to assess lead quality before passing it to the next group. By establishing a quality checkpoint before each handoff, you isolate some of the variables in your funnel, which helps you diagnose issues later on. For example, if problems arise in converting leads to opportunities, then you know to focus either on checkpoints 1 or 2. However, if win rates are a problem, then the issue probably falls on or after checkpoint 3.

A well-structured SLA ensures every team has a clear checkpoint for confirming lead quality before handing the prospect over to the next team. Clearly defined and consistently managed checkpoints improve forecasting accuracy and create predictability in pipeline generation.

CEO ROLE

The SLA Decision requires teams to break down siloes and coordinate in new ways. The CEO should nominate the sales leader and marketing leader to co-own the SLA Workshop sessions and the resulting *Revenue Operations Playbook.*

Your role is to ensure all stakeholders are aligned and committed to the process. You can do this by requesting a read-out of the *Revenue Operations Playbook* at the end of the workshop to check commitment. During the read-out, listen for, and address, any potential conflicts or misalignment before the SLA is executed (see Chapter 9).

As CEO, you may not be tactical enough to make some of these decisions, but you need to develop a basic understanding of the lead management infrastructure being built. When your company looks to exit, investors expect you and your team to be able to articulate how these pieces fit together in the detailed way that a diligence process requires.

As CEO, your role in the SLA process is to:

- **Champion urgency and remove roadblocks,** such as resource constraints or resistance from leadership to participate. Prioritize the leaders' time to get these decisions made quickly. Once factors are prioritized, the SLA Workshop and resulting decisions can be made in a matter of days.
- **Kick-off Session #2, *Codify the SLA*,** with the cross-functional team. Use your presence to reinforce urgency, break down silos, and frame the SLA as a critical enabler of scalable growth.
- **Request a Read-Out** of the Revenue Operations Playbook. Ensure the leaders from Sales, Marketing, and RevOps are present and listen for potential conflict and misalignment. Critically review the SLA decision made to ensure you understand how the components fit together well enough to explain back to investors when needed.

COMMON CEO MISTAKE: PROCEEDING WITHOUT REVOPS AND SALES TRAINING PRESENT

This workshop is meaningless if it isn't executed. In this case, execution means building out the systems and training the Reps. Ensure the person responsible for the build and the person responsible for training sales are fully engaged in the workshop. Their input is critical to designing a process that can be built, enforced, and adopted. They need to understand the context behind why these decisions were made to configure systems accurately and explain the process clearly to Reps.

Many earlier growth stage companies do not have a full-time sales trainer. If you do not yet have a designated sales trainer, then look to nominate someone, such as the Sales Manager or Product Marketer, to take on that role for this exercise.

Once you've confirmed the four required participants (your sales and marketing leaders, RevOps lead (or build partner), and the person responsible for sales training), you're ready to host the workshop that brings it all together. Step 7 is the SLA Workshop, a focused two-day sprint that aligns Sales, Marketing, and RevOps on a shared process to convert leads to pipeline.

STEP 7: SLA WORKSHOP

Owner: *Sales Leader and Marketing Leader,* **Duration:** *2 Days (Days 67–68)*

The SLA Workshop is a series of working sessions that can be conducted with a one- or two-day agenda. This section lays out the mechanics of each session: the participants, the decisions to make, the agenda, and the resulting page in the Revenue Operations Playbook.

Session #1: Define Lead Stages (1 Hour)

1. **Attendees:** Sales leader, marketing leader, BDR lead, RevOps lead, sales trainer. For this session, either the marketing or sales leader can lead the discussion.
2. **Decisions to Make:**
   a. **Lead Stage Naming** (e.g., MQL, SQL, SAO, SQO)
   b. **Exit Criteria** for each stage
   c. **Record Type** (Lead vs. Contact vs. Opportunity)
   d. **CRM Stage & Pipeline Percentage** (e.g., SQO = Stage 3, 15% pipeline weight)
   e. **Owner** (e.g., Marketing, BDR, AE)

Scan Code for Downloadable Template

FIGURE 22: "Define Lead Stages" Session Agenda

Duration	Agenda	Owner	Attendees
10 min.	**Set Objectives:** This session is the leadership kick-off to the two-day workshop. Aligning on these stages together in the room models how they want their teams to work together for the next two days, with live discussion, healthy debate, and codification of decisions.	Sales or Marketing Leader	• Head of Sales • Head of Marketing • Head of BDRs • RevOps Lead • Sales Trainer
25 min.	**Codify Lead Stages:** Compare your lead stages to the stages provided in this book. Ensure you have a qualification stage that happens before handing off to the BDRs and another before opening pipeline.		
25 min.	**Define Key Stage Elements:** Capture the record type (lead, contact, account, opportunity), CRM stages (stage 0, 1, 2, 3,) and pipeline-weighted percentage (0%, 10%, etc.) for stages that progress in the CRM.		

Using the inbound lead stages provided in Chapter 7, the output from this session may look like Figure 23, which would be included as the first page in your *Revenue Operations Playbook.*

Now that your team has defined the lead qualification stages, they are ready to define what lead quality means and establish the process they will follow to graduate prospects from one stage to the next until pipeline is opened.

FIGURE 23: Revenue Operations Playbook
Page 1 Example: Lead Qualification Stages

Lead Stages	Pipeline Stages	CRM Record Type	Owner	Exit Criteria
Lead		Lead	Marketing	MKTG Lead Captured (form fill, webinar registration, download, etc.)
MQL		Lead	Marketing	MKTG Scored Lead
SQL		Account + Contact	BDR	BDR Qualifies Lead & Books Initial Sales Meeting
SAO	Stage 0: 0%	Opportunity	Rep	AE Hand-Off/Validates Will Hold the Initial Sales Meeting
SQO	Stage 1: 15%	Opportunity	Rep	AE Meeting Held/Confirms Buyer Intent (BANT)

Session #2: Codify the SLA (4 Hours)

1. **Attendees:** Sales leader, marketing leader, BDR lead, RevOps lead, 1 or 2 sales reps, demand generation lead, sales trainer
2. **Decisions to Make:**
   a. **Lead Qualification Criteria** required to book the initial sales meeting (and convert to SQL) and open pipeline (and convert to SQO)
   b. **SLA Rules of Engagement** for lead status, Rep actions, rejection, recycle, closed-lost reasons, and timing allowed for each stage.

The output from the first half of the session would look something like Figure 25 and would be included as the second page in your *Revenue Operations Playbook.*

FIGURE 24: "Codify the SLA" Session Agenda

<table>
<tr><th>Duration</th><th>Agenda</th><th>Owner</th><th>Attendees</th></tr>
<tr><td>10 min.</td><td>CEO Kick-Off: Champion the importance of clarity, consensus, and commitment to the new process.</td><td>CEO</td><td rowspan="5">• Head of Sales
• Head of Marketing
• BDR Manager
• 1-2 Sales Reps (Reps on the phones)
• Demand Generation Lead
• RevOps Lead
• Sales Trainer</td></tr>
<tr><td>20 min.</td><td>Review Lead Stages: Introduce the team to funnel stage definitions codified in the previous session.</td><td rowspan="3">Sales or Marketing Leader</td></tr>
<tr><td>1.5 hours</td><td>Define SQL Criteria/Minimum Criteria to Book the First Sales Meeting: Identify the minimum qualification criteria a prospect needs to meet to book the initial sales meeting (i.e., firmographics, demographics, technographics).</td></tr>
<tr><td>2 hours</td><td>Establish SLA Rules of Engagement: Define the following for each stage:
• Lead Status: CRM field indicating progress (e.g., Working, Disqualified).
• Required Actions: Rep expectations for progressing leads (e.g., BDR must attempt 10 touches over 14 days, including 3 phone calls).
• Minimum Criteria to Open Pipeline: What does the prospect need to prove to warrant further conversions (e.g., AE must confirm BANT before converting SAO to SQO).
• Rejection, Recycle, Closed-Lost Reasons: CRM dropdown options for lead disposition (e.g., Unable to Reach).
• Stage Timing: Maximum duration before a lead must be recycled or closed (e.g., BDR must complete 10 touches in 15 days).</td></tr>
</table>

FIGURE 25: Revenue Operations Playbook
Page 2 Example: Lead Quality Criteria Definition

	SQL Criteria	Defined
Quality Criteria	Job Title	Radiologist, Front Office Manager, IT Manager
	Job Seniority	Owner, Manager
	Geography	USA, UK Only
Exit Criteria		Schedules Initial Sales Meeting

The second half of the session codifies the process behind which Reps will move leads from initial sales meeting booked to opening pipeline.

Now that the team knows what to look for related to lead quality, they are ready to walk through the stages and detail the components needed to progress a lead. The SLA picks up once a lead is routed to a BDR by the MAP. For each stage following, the team will use this session to map:

- **Process Step:** What the rep is doing
- **CRM Status:** What CRM status will be used for that process step
- **Required Actions:** Rep instructions for things they must do in that step
- **Rejection, Recycle, and Closed-Lost Reasons:** When it is a quality checkpoint, what reasons are available for rep to reject or recycle the lead
- **Timing:** How long the lead is allowed to stay in that process step

A Note About Minimum Criteria to Open Pipeline

When defining the minimum criteria to open pipeline and convert to SQO, you're no longer asking *Is this the type of account we would sell to?* because that's already been addressed twice in earlier MQL and SQL stages. Now, you're qualifying whether the buyer is *actively in-market* and worth the Rep's time to try to advance through the pipeline.

This qualification should align with your sales methodology and must include a scheduled follow-up. For example, if your team uses BANT (Budget, Authority, Need, Timing), the rep should confirm those details during the first sales meeting and book a next step. Scheduling the follow-up meeting becomes the trigger to convert the opportunity to a Sales-Qualified Opportunity (SQO) and open pipeline.

The example output in Figure 26 illustrates a codified SLA for just one quality checkpoint, from BDR receiving a scored lead, to qualifying the prospect and scheduling the initial sales meeting. Your SLA will include the next checkpoint, when the AE opens pipeline. Both represent page three of your *Revenue Operations Playbook*.

FIGURE 26: Revenue Operations Playbook
Page 3 Example: BDR SLA for Working an MQL

Step	Funnel Stage	Process Step	SFDC Status	Required Action	Rejection/Recycle Reasons	Timing
1	MQL	Lead Converts to MQL	New	Lead meets Score threshold of 100 in HubSpot and is synced to Salesforce as a Contact record with Tasks assigned. BDRs will be assigned by HubSpot.	—	Eyeball accept/ reject < 2 hours
		BDR Rejects	Rejected	BDR rejects bad leads that will not be worked and not nurtured.	• Bad Data • Duplicate Record • Requested Support • Employee • Competitor	
		BD Accepts	Working	BDR is responsible for 10 touches over 10 days to ensure the lead meets the definition of an SQL. Touches include emails, phone calls, and LinkedIn Outreach. Initial contact must be made within 48 hours; for "hot leads," initial contact must be attempted within 24 hours. Hot leads are defined as: • Demo Request • Inbound Chat	—	10 touches over 10 days, initial contact within 24–48 hours
		BDR Disqualifies	Recycled	AE hand-off/validates will hold the initial sales meeting	• Poor Product Fit • No Need/Urgency • Unable to Reach	
2	SQL	BDR Converts to SQL	Stage 0: SQL 0% Opportunity	AE meeting held/confirms buyer intent (BANT)	—	Convert to Stage 0 on qualification

Once your team has defined the steps, required actions, timing, and recycle reasons for each stage leading to open pipeline and have agreed on the minimum criteria to book a meeting and to open pipeline, then you're ready to move on to lead scoring.

The qualification criteria required to book the first meeting will become the basis for your lead-score logic. When done this way, lead scoring is better informed to surface and route the best-fit leads to sales at scale.

SLA Workshop Session #3: Map Lead Score (1.5 Hours)

1. **Attendees:** Marketing leader, BDR lead, RevOps lead, demand generation lead
2. **Decisions to Make:**
   a. **Lead Score Logic** to prioritize and route leads to sales based on buyer fit attributes (e.g., demographics, firmographics, technographics) and buyer interest attributes (e.g., ebook downloads, demo requests, event attendance)
   b. **Data Enrichment Opportunities** to sync with the MAP that append buyer fit traits, thus reducing the number of fields on a standard form

LEAD SCORING IS YOUR FIRST QUALIFICATION CHECKPOINT

Lead scoring is the logic the MAP uses to know whether the lead is ready to be qualified by a Rep or needs further engagement with Marketing to build interest first. The logic is based on culminating scores on a lead until it reaches a lead-threshold number. A lead threshold is the total score a lead needs to reach to trigger the MAP and route the lead to a Rep.

Lead scoring is your company's first attempt to measure sales readiness of a lead. Scoring occurs instantly at the time the lead is captured online as a form fill, webinar registrant, or demo request or in batches when leads are uploaded to MAP from an event or other list. It automates the process of screening individuals who exhibit both the *minimum criteria to book a meeting* traits and the online buyer signals (collected by the MAP) that can indicate early signs of sales readiness, such as visiting the pricing page or attending a webinar. Each trait and signal is assigned a score

FIGURE 27: "Map Lead Score" Session Agenda

Scan Code for Downloadable Template

Duration	Agenda	Owner	Attendees
5 min.	**Set Lead Score Threshold:** If unknown, start with 100.	Marketing leader	• Head of Marketing • BDR Manager • Demand Generation Lead • RevOps Lead • Sales Trainer
15 min.	**Weight Buyer Fit and Buyer Interest Category Scores:** Consider weighing Buyer Fit at 40% and Buyer Interest at 60% of the lead-score threshold to start.		
10 min.	**Define Buyer Fit Attributes:** Carry over the traits identified as the minimum criteria to book a meeting to score against.		
5 min.	**Enrich Buyer Fit Fields:** Once the fit traits are defined, identify any fields that can be populated through the MAP or via an API with a contact enrichment platform.		
25 min.	**Map Buyer Fit Scores:** Within each trait, list the selections that will appear on the lead capture form. Note the max score allowed for each trait and score the options up to that max score.		
25 min.	**Define Buyer Interest Actions:** Identify the actions that should trigger a score, such as content download, website engagement, email engagement, and others.		
5 min.	**Define "Hot Leads" to Bypass Scoring:** These are leads that Sales will want to talk to right away regardless of scoring.		

that accumulates over time. Once the lead reaches the scoring threshold, typically around 100 points, it's automatically routed to a BDR or Sales Rep for qualification.

A common misconception about lead scoring is that it qualifies a lead. Lead scoring does not qualify a lead; instead, it *prioritizes* a lead for a Rep to qualify. Lead scoring is inherently fallible as an indicator of "quality" because it is both based on our best guess for what signals imply sales readiness and relies on the truthfulness of the prospect when filling out a form.

You make this trade-off on precision in lead scoring to accommodate scale. The purpose of lead scoring with a MAP is to automate the screening process at scale, so hundreds and thousands of leads can be inspected in real-time with the best-looking leads identified and prioritized for sales to qualify.

Consider the process for screening a list of leads from a recent event without lead scoring. When done manually, screening becomes inconsistent, and Sales can get overloaded with calling on prospects who may or may not be a fit for a sales discussion. Leads get lost, Sales gets frustrated, and Marketing gets a bad reputation for sending "poor quality" leads.

Mapping the lead score is dependent on two inputs from earlier exercises.

- **From SLA Workshop Session #2:** The logic behind the lead score is based on the minimum criteria to book a meeting defined in the previous Codify the SLA session. The lead score logic is Marketing's filter to ensure leads passed to Sales for qualification are meeting these minimum requirements, at least on paper.
- **From the ICP:** You may also configure the model to score leads from A accounts higher than those from B, C, or D tiers (see Chapter 5, Step 5).

While most teams begin with a static scoring model based on these inputs, AI-powered scoring engines can later enhance this logic by identifying which traits and signals correlate most strongly with higher conversion. Your initial lead-scoring logic gives AI models a strong foundation to learn from once you've built it out in your MAP and have started to collect data.

BUYER FIT AND BUYER INTEREST

Lead scores are made up of two broad categories: buyer fit and buyer interest. Buyer fit relates to the demographics and firmographics that combine to make the prospect look like a good-fit customer (e.g., job title in an account of a certain size). Buyer interest is those online signals the MAP can read

FIGURE 28: Buyer Fit Scoring Example: Job Seniority

Job Seniority	Max Score
Owner	10
C-Level / Executive	10
VP / Director	8
Manager	8
Individual Contributor	5
Entry Level	3
Intern	1
Consultant	0

that may indicate the prospect is engaged and ready to talk with Sales (e.g., asset download).

Each category has a number of traits to score against. For example, buyer fit traits could include job title, seniority, and vertical. Buyer interest traits may include asset download, email clicks, and webinar attendance. Each trait itself contains a range of options. Lead scoring relates to scoring on that range of options. For example, the scores for job seniority may look like Figure 28.

If you are following the 100-Day Plan sequence, base the buyer fit scores on traits defined as the qualification criteria required to book the first sales meeting in the previous SLA session and account scoring from Chapter 5. If you are not following the activities of the 100-Day Plan, you can skip the account scoring inputs and focus instead on the minimum criteria as the primary input to book the meeting. Defining the minimum criteria to book a meeting is required to map an adequate lead score.

Once you have mapped the lead-score logic, you'll add the resulting scoring matrix in Figure 29 as page 4 of your *Revenue Operations Playbook*.

Now that the team has set the lead scoring logic, it's time to turn their attention to tracking and attribution reporting.

FIGURE 29: Revenue Operations Playbook
Page 4 Example: Lead Score Map

Buyer Interest: 60% of total		Buyer Fit: 40% of Total (based on SQL definition in SLA)			
Engagement (select all that apply)		Demographics (select 1-3 questions)		Firmagraphics (select 1-2 questions)	
Hot Leads Defined in SLA. Send to sales regardless of buyer fit.	Max Score 100	**Job Title** Based on MQL definition.	Max Score 10	**Company Revenue** Optional: May remove if asking about employee size.	Max Score 10
Get a Demo Request	100	HR	10	$500+ Million	0
Contact Us Form	100	IT	10	$10-500 Million	0
Free Trial Registration	100	Safety	10	$1-10 Million	0
DL of XYZ (optional per SLA)	100	Risk	10	$500k-$1 Million	0
		Administrator	7	$250k-$500k	10
All Other Leads Points are cumulative. Remove criteria which doesn't apply.	Max Score 75	CHRO	10	$100k-$250k	10
Content Download		Sales Support	2	$50k-$100k	10
DL of Highest Value Content XYZ	75	Other Support	2	$10k-50k	10
DL of High Value Content XYZ	60	Dental Assistant	1	Less Than $10k	5
DL of Mid-Level Content XYZ	50	Hygienist	1	**Employee Count** Optional: May remove if asking about company revenue	Max Score 10
		Lap Manager	1	1000+ Employees	10
ROI Tool		Sales	1	201-1000 Employees	8
Registers for ROI Tool	50	Marketing	1	51-200 Employees	6
Downloads ROI Tool	20	Training	1	2-50 Employees	5
Uses ROI Tool	10	Service Technician	1	Self-Employed	0
		Sales	1		

SLA Workshop Session #4: Set Attribution Rules (2 Hours)

1. **Attendees:** Sales leader, marketing leader, RevOps lead, BDR lead, partner lead, demand generation Lead
2. **Decisions to Make:**
   a. **Naming Convention** for lead sources or channels (e.g., event, website) to be standardized in the CRM and used by Partners and Marketing in their tracking systems
   b. **Attribution Rules of Engagement** for each team for when they can select a lead source to the CRM
   c. **Additional Lead Detail Fields** (optional) to include, which enable the CRM to become a source of truth tracking for all teams (e.g., publisher, content)

Scan Code for Downloadable Template

FIGURE 30: "Set Attribution Rules" Session Agenda

Duration	Agenda	Owner	Attendees
30 min.	**Standardize CRM Naming Convention for Lead Sources:** Lead sources represent the channels where a lead was captured (e.g., social, email, event, outbound). Standardize the lead source selection options available in the CRM.	Marketing Leader	• Head of Sales • Head of Marketing • BDR Manager • Demand Generation Lead • Partner Lead • RevOps Lead • Sales Trainer
20 min.	**Establish Lead Source Rules of Engagement:** Identify the lead sources that will auto-append from the MAP, and which lead source options will be available for Reps to select and when.		
30 min.	**Identify Additional Lead Detail Fields (optional):** needed in the CRM to enable it to be become a source of truth tracking for all teams (e.g., event name, first-touch content name)		
20 min.	**Standardize the CRM Campaign Naming Convention:** to align campaign tracking across the different tracking platforms used by marketing, sales, and partners (e.g., YYYYMM_CampaignName)		
20 min.	**Define the URL tracking parameters:** to be used by Marketing in other tracking systems and align those with the new naming conventions.		

d. **CRM Campaign Naming Convention** to unify campaign tracking across tracking platforms used by Marketing, Sales, and Channel Partners

By the end of this discussion, the team will have detailed the naming conventions, required fields, input sources if outside the CRM, and campaign name naming convention for wide use among the commercial teams. The output of this session will become page 5 of the *Revenue Operations Playbook* (see Figure 31).

Now that the team has committed to a process to track attribution and ROI throughout a variety of lead generation sources, it's time to wrap up the workshop with a discussion about centralizing email and compliance.

FIGURE 31: Revenue Operations Playbook
Page 5 Example: Attribution Rules

Salesforce Dimensions	Lead Source (SFDC) / Medium (GA)	Lead Detail 1: Publisher
Required	Required	Required
Input Source	Mapped from UTM_Medium for digital or BDR manual Select	Mapped from UTM_Source for digital or BDR manual select
Field Type in SFDC	Drop Down	Drop Down
Examples	*social (appended from UTM)*	Partner Name (Drop Down)
	email (appended from UTM)	List Source Name (Drop Down)
	affiliates (appended from UTM)	Event Name (Drop Down)
	referral (appended from UTM)	
	paidsearch (appended from UTM)	
	display (appended from UTM)	
	Website Chat	
	Webinar	
	Event	
	Outbound	
	Inbound Phone	
	Partner	

SLA Workshop Session #5: Centralize Email Process (1 Hour)

1. **Attendees:** Sales leader, marketing leader, customer success leader, RevOps lead, email lead, BDR lead, demand generation lead
2. **Decisions to Make:**
    a. **Opt-in rules** based on regional compliance regulations
    b. **Opt-out processes** for Marketing, Sales, BDR, and CS to follow
    c. **Standard suppression rules** and files to be used
    d. **Designated email lead** to oversee the opt-in/opt-out process, email calendars, messaging, and performance of email as a channel

FIGURE 32: "Centralize Email Process" Session Agenda

Scan Code for Downloadable Template

Duration	Agenda	Owner	Attendees
15 min.	**Email Types:** Align on the types of emails to be centralized (e.g., BDR sequences, marketing nurtures, etc.).	Email Lead	• Head of Sales • Head of Marketing • BDR Manager • Demand Generation Lead • Partner Lead • RevOps Lead • Sales Trainer
45 min.	For each email type, define: • **Regions:** Identify the regions relevant to the different types of emails, Audience Type - Net New Lists (e.g., outbound), Leads (e.g., inbound), Referrals (e.g., partners), Expansion Leads (e.g., customer success) • **Audience Sources:** Can be MAP, CRM, Partners, or Data Enrichment Platforms • **Standard Suppressions:** At a minimum, companies should suppress opt-outs. • **Email Platform:** Different email types may be sent from different tools. • **Frequency:** Generally based on a per week send (e.g., 1 email every 2 weeks). • **Opt-In Policy:** Most countries outside of the US require either an explicit opt-in or a double opt-in. In the US, most, but not all, states allow an implied opt-in. • **Email Owner:** Whether all email types are managed by a single owner or managed independently on the teams, identify the name of the point of contact		

WHY CENTRALIZE YOUR EMAILS

Nearly three-quarters of companies rely on email as a primary source of leads.[4] Although a critical channel to protect, it is also the one channel most susceptible to poor or uncoordinated execution. At any point, up to five teams, including Marketing, Sales, BDRs, Partners, and Customer Success, could be vying to use the CRM database to send promotional emails. When each team manages their own email calendar, develops their own messaging, and oversees their own compliance with regulations for promotional emails, it can put the company at risk of getting blacklisted (marked as a spammer and unable to reach the inbox), endanger performance, and frustrate buyers.

Centralizing the email process is one way CEOs can protect the reputation of the company's brand, improve performance of a top channel, and ensure buyers and customers have a positive experience. Three types of promotional emails can be centralized.

- **Single Promo:** a singular email or short series of emails with a targeted message and an end date, like an invitation to an upcoming webinar.
- **Ongoing Series:** a triggered email sequence meant to engage prospects over a longer period of time, like BDR outreach sequences or Marketing nurtures.
- **Third-Pary Emails:** an external email sent on behalf of the company by a third-party advertiser or partner, most often leveraged by the Marketing or the Partner team.

Transactional emails (those that are not promotional in nature) are account-related messages like release notes or transaction receipts. These are generally managed by Product or Customer Success. They adhere to different regional compliance regulations and are therefore generally not centralized.

Centralizing the email process starts with the decision to align all promotional emails under a single owner, usually someone from the

4 KBCM Sapphire SaaS Survey 2024

Marketing team. When one person oversees the email channel, efficiencies can be found in multiple places. The company is better equipped to improve targeting and conversion rate on offers, align messaging with branding, and maintain consistent compliance to spam regulations.

A single owner provides the company with a lever to improve conversions through testing and tooling. If the email channel cannot roll up under a single owner, then nominate and empower a person from each stakeholder team (Sales, Marketing, Partners, and Customer Success) to form an email council where each function aligns with centralized messaging, a unified delivery calendar, and a singular opt-in/opt-out process that adheres to regional regulations.

Once your team understands who is in charge of email delivery, they are ready to make the key decisions needed to inform the systems in support of a centralized process.

Scribe the decisions from this meeting and include as page 6 of your *Revenue Operations Playbook* (see Figure 33).

This session concludes the SLA Workshop. By its end, your team will have codified six critical pages of your *Revenue Operations Playbook*, each one detailing the processes your teams will follow and how your systems must be built to support them.

Now that your team has aligned with the five core SLA Decisions and codified them into your *Revenue Operations Playbook*, it's time to put them into action.

FIGURE 33: Revenue Operations Playbook
Page 6 Example: Centralized Email Process

	Single Promo	Ongoing Series	Third-Party
Description	Single email or series of emails with a start and end date	Email series with no end date	Singular emails sent via a 3rd party on our behalf or to a 3rd-party list
Audience	Prospects	Targets / Prospects	Targets
List Source Examples	• Existing Database or Channel Partner List	• BDR Identifies Contact in Zoominfo • Marketing receives list from a trade show	• One-Time List Purchase • One-Time Co-Marketing Promo to Partner List
Suppressions	• Unsubscribes • No Contacts • Existing Customers • Nurtures/Outreach Recipients	• Unsubscribes • No Contacts • Existing Customers • Single Promo Emails in same week	• Unsubscribes • No Contacts • Existing Customers
Example	Marketing Offer: Webinar Invite, Booth Presence	BDR Prospecting/ Marketing Nurture	Sponsored Email
Responsible Function	Marketing	All Under Marketing	Marketing
Tech	HubSpot	Outreach/HubSpot	3rd-Party Tool
Delivery Schedule	No restriction, but good reason for more than 2 per week	1x every 2 weeks	3rd-Party Schedule
Geographies	USA & CA	USA & CA	USA & CA
Out-In Policy	Implied Opt-In	Implied Opt-In	Explicit Opt-in
Point of Contact	Jane Smith in Marketing	Jane Smith in Marketing	Jane Smith in Marketing

EXECUTIVE SUMMARY 9

HOW CEOS EXECUTE THE SLA DECISION

Key Takeaways

- **SLA Decision Execution Depends on Systems & Training**
  The SLA is meaningless without roll-out. Execution happens in two ways: systems built to support the new process and Reps trained to use it.
- **SLA Systems Build = Revenue Infrastructure**
  Building the SLA Decisions into your CRM and MAP creates a shared commercial infrastructure that enables more accurate forecasting and clean handoffs between teams resulting in predictable pipeline and revenue.
- **SLA Execution Sets the Baseline for AI Accuracy**
  The more structured your CRM and MAP structure are around lead stages, timing, and attribution, the more accurate and actionable your AI features and insights will be.
- **Training Isn't Enough; Sales Managers Need to Enforce**
  Rep training ensures every BDR and AE understands the new process and why it's a priority, but training alone will not be enough. Sales Managers need to reinforce the new behaviors in their weekly 1:1s with real-time alerting and governance reports.

Chapter 9 Deliverables

By the end of this 31-day execution phase, your company will have:

- A Fully Operational Revenue Operations Playbook
- CRM and MAP Systems Built as "Source of Truth" Reporting
- Sales Reps Trained and Certified on the SLA
- Performance Monitoring and Alerts in Place
- Structured Data for Forecasting and Future AI

Why Executing the SLA Matters

Revenue growth isn't just a function of sales performance, but a result of disciplined, coordinated GTM execution. Once you build the SLA decisions into your CRM and MAP, you connect rep performance to campaign performance in a measurable way. This is a powerful milestone in your team's transformation journey. This connection unlocks the data and insights they'll need to scale wins or diagnose problems to create a predictable pipeline.

So much of the success of the SLA Decisions your team has made rests on the Reps' ability to follow the SLA. Training Reps and holding them accountable to the new process is critical for implementation. Without adherence to the process, leads can struggle to convert to pipeline and the data in your CRM can become incomplete, making your CRM unreliable for diagnostics or forecasting.

9

HOW CEOS EXECUTE THE SLA DECISION

DURATION: 31 DAYS FOR EXECUTION (DAYS 69–100)

WITH SLA DECISIONS finalized and documented in your Revenue Operations Playbook, it's time to execute. Over the next 31 days, your teams will build the systems and train the people to embed those decisions into the daily process, ensuring that Sales, Marketing, and RevOps operate as a single, coordinated engine. Execution includes two key steps:

- Systems Build (30 Days)
- Certified Rep Training (1 Day)

This chapter outlines what CEOs should expect as their teams integrate the SLA into the company's core go-to-market infrastructure. Execution in this phase includes operationalizing the lead scoring logic, attribution reporting rules, email workflows, CRM and MAP configuration, rep enablement, and reporting dashboards that came out of the workshop.

CEO ROLE

As CEO, your job during execution is to reinforce urgency and remove blockers. Empower your RevOps lead and Sales Trainer with the resources needed to build systems quickly and to ensure Reps are trained and certified before re-engaging with live calls.

What Good SLA Execution Looks Like to CEOs

- SLA and lead qualification process documented in the Revenue Operations Playbook.
- Systems configured based on SLA Decisions; enriched data applied where possible.
- Stage timing and funnel progression visible via dashboards, alerts, and manager oversight.
- Email process centralized and documented in the playbook.
- Reps trained, certified, and held accountable to SLA timing expectations.

Executing the SLA Decisions from your workshop begins with the systems build. As CEO, you don't need to manage the details, but you do need to know what to look for so you can provide helpful oversight to keep the team accountable.

STEP 8: SYSTEMS BUILD (CRM & MAP)

Owner: *RevOps Leader,* **Duration:** *30 Days (Days 69–99)*

Now that your SLA Decisions are codified in the Revenue Operations Playbook, it's time to configure your CRM and MAP systems to support them. Over the next 30 days, your RevOps leader, or a trusted build partner, will translate lead stages, qualification logic, attribution rules, and email workflows into structured processes that support lead progression and enforce coordination across teams.

The steps that follow are designed to serve as a checklist covering the common elements required to enable reliable reporting, clean handoffs,

SLA EXECUTION SETS THE BASELINE FOR AI ACCURACY

It can be tempting to turn on the AI features in your tools right away. *Resist this urge until these SLA foundations are in place.* While this build is manual and rule-based, it creates the structure your AI needs to drive smarter execution.

Most modern sales and marketing platforms offer AI-driven lead scoring, attribution, and rep coaching based on historical patterns, but the AI is only as good as the data it's fed. The more structured your CRM and MAP structure are based on lead stages, timing, and attribution, the more accurate and actionable your AI features and insights will be. Skip this step and you risk AI outputs becoming noisy or misleading.

and AI readiness. Your exact build may vary slightly based on your systems, expect to personalize where needed, but prioritize speed, accuracy, and completeness with your team.

1. **Lead Qualification Stages and Record Types**
   The system build begins with aligning your MAP and CRM to the qualification stages defined in your SLA Workshop.
   - ☐ **Platform Sync:** Ensure the MAP and CRM have a real-time bi-directional sync.
   - ☐ **Record Type:** Map each qualification stage (e.g., MQL, SQL, SAO, SQO) to the right object type (Lead, Contact, Opportunity).
   - ☐ **CRM Stage & Pipeline Percentage:** Align any opportunity stage to CRM pipeline stages and weighted percentages (e.g., SQO = Stage 3, 15%).
   - ☐ **Lead Status Fields:** Create and implement the designated lead status fields (e.g., Working, Disqualified) to track progress.

- [ ] **Rep Tasks:** Build auto-assigned tasks (e.g., BDR must update lead status to SQL within 1 hour of logging the first meeting).
- [ ] **Disposition Reasons:** Update rejection, recycle, and closed-lost reason dropdowns (e.g., "Unable to Reach").

2. **SLA Timing and Governance**

   Operationalize the timing expectations between stages in your CRM.

   - [ ] **Stage Timing:** Automatically stamp the date when a lead enters each stage to enable time-in-stage tracking.
   - [ ] **CRM Alerts:** Set up alerts to notify Sales Managers when leads exceed SLA timing thresholds (e.g., send an alert on Day 16 if the SLA allows 15 days in stage).
   - [ ] **Progression Governance Reports:** Build reports for Sales Managers to track:
     - ↳ **Time to First Contact:** *Are reps reaching out fast enough to meet SLA timing?*
     - ↳ **Rejection & Recycle Rates:** *Are leads being recycled with valid reasons?*
     - ↳ **Time in Stage:** *Are leads progressing on pace, or getting stuck in stage?*
     - ↳ **Stalled Leads:** *Which leads are stalled and require coaching with the Rep?*

3. **Lead Score Logic**

   Translate your scoring model into system logic to route leads.

   - [ ] **Buyer Fit & Buyer Interest:** Configure MAP scoring fields based on traits and behaviors defined in the workshop.
   - [ ] **Lead Routing:** Set routing rules to trigger handoffs to Reps once a score threshold is met.
   - [ ] **Data Enrichment:** Connect enrichment tools to auto-fill key fields (e.g., industry, employee count, geography).

4. **Attribution Rules**
   Standardize how attribution is tracked and reported.
   - ☐ **Lead Source Naming:** Provide drop-down lead source options for Reps to select.
   - ☐ **Lead Detail Fields:** Add custom attribution fields (e.g., "Content," "Audience Source") as needed.
   - ☐ **CRM Campaign Naming:** Enforce CRM campaign naming conventions among teams.
   - ☐ **URL Tracking Parameters:** Ensure all links include UTMs that match the attribution structure.

5. **Centralized Email Process**
   Email execution depends on reliable audience lists and legal compliance.
   - ☐ **Audience Lists:** Create segmented audience lists to support outbound, inbound, partner referrals, expansion.
   - ☐ **List Sources:** Automate list syncs where possible; define manual upload process for offline lists (like events).
   - ☐ **Suppressions:** Build logic for suppression lists tied to opt-outs or status changes.
   - ☐ **Workflows:** Set up campaign workflows for single promo and ongoing series with send logic defined in the workshop.
   - ☐ **Opt-In Compliance:** Ensure checkbox on the form and legal footer in place for explicit opt-in and email workflow set-up for double opt-in; review privacy policy with legal.
   - ☐ **Opt-Out Handling:** Add CRM fields for Reps and Marketing to manually opt out contacts; automate self-serve unsubscribes via email footer links.

Once the systems are configured and the workflows in place, the final step is to ensure Reps know how to use them. Step 9 focuses on training your sales team to understand and follow the new SLA process.

STEP 9: CERTIFIED REP TRAINING

Owner: *Sales Trainer,* **Duration:** *1 Day (Days 99–100)*

There are two ways to operationalize your SLA: Build the systems and train the people. Now that your CRM and MAP have been configured to support the SLA, it's time to train your teams on the processes they'll follow and the systems they'll use to support them.

This one-day session introduces the new workflow, clarifies role expectations, and outlines how rep performance will be governed from this point onward. Sales is responsible not only for ensuring the training is

FIGURE 34: SLA Training Agenda

<table>
<tr><th>Duration</th><th>Agenda</th><th>Owner</th><th>Attendees</th></tr>
<tr><td>10 min.</td><td>Champion the SLA: Kick-Off, Decision Recap</td><td>CEO</td><td rowspan="6">• BDRs
• AEs
• Marketing</td></tr>
<tr><td>30 min.</td><td>Lead Stages & Roles: Lead Stage Ownership, 3 Quality Checkpoints, Record Types</td><td rowspan="7">Sales Trainer</td></tr>
<tr><td>45 min.</td><td>SLA Workflow & Rules of Engagement: Qualification Criteria, Lead Status & Stage Actions, Timing Expectations</td></tr>
<tr><td>45 min.</td><td>Lead Score Logic: Buyer Fit & Interest, Routing Rules, Form Enrichment</td></tr>
<tr><td>30 min.</td><td>Attribution Rules: Lead Source Naming, Lead Detail Fields, CRM Campaign Naming</td></tr>
<tr><td>30 min.</td><td>Email Process: Email Lead, Opt-In Rules, Opt-Out Process, Email Calendar</td></tr>
<tr><td>30 min.</td><td>Performance Metrics & Monitoring: CRM Alerts, Sales Manager Oversight, Continuous Feedback</td><td rowspan="2">• BDRs
• AEs</td></tr>
<tr><td>20 min.</td><td>Rep Certification: Lead Scenarios, SLA Timing Quiz, Disposition Matching
Reps should be tested and certified by the end of the session, not just exposed to the material.</td></tr>
</table>

delivered, but also for reinforcing adherence to the process through alerts, reporting, and coaching after the rollout.

Plan to kick off the session briefly yourself. The teams need to hear that SLA adoption is a priority from the top.

The example agenda in Figure 34 illustrates a structured, one-day SLA training session. It outlines the recommended topics, timing, and owners to guide your Sales Trainer in delivering a consistent, effective rollout.

Rep Certification Examples

Before returning to the sales floor, expect Reps to pass a short certification to confirm comprehension:

- **Lead Scenarios:** Test three lead profiles for reps to qualify or disqualify.
- **SLA Timing Quiz:** Fill in the blanks (e.g., time to first contact = ___ hours).
- **Disposition Matching:** Rejection vs. Recycle vs. Closed-Lost by stage.

POST-TRAINING GOVERNANCE

Training is not a one-and-done event. After the session, expect sales leaders to reinforce SLA adherence through active governance. Two tools created during the systems build support this:

- **Real-Time Alerts:** triggered when Reps fail to make first contact within the SLA window.
- **Progression Governance Reports:** weekly dashboards showing how long leads sit in each stage, flagging SLA breaches for manager follow-up.

Hold your sales leader accountable for SLA governance just as you would for pipeline reviews. Request these tools be woven into the Sales manager's regular 1:1s, coaching, and performance reviews. Reps who consistently miss SLA timing should receive additional coaching. Team-wide misses may indicate a need for process review to gauge whether the SLA is proving unrealistic.

By the end of these 31 days, you should have a fully operational SLA built into your systems, understood by your Reps, and governed by your managers.

With your SLA now embedded in both systems and processes, you are ready to measure where it's working and where it may be breaking down.

EXECUTIVE SUMMARY 10

HOW CEOS MEASURE THE SLA DECISION

Key Takeaways

- **Pipeline Health Is Visible in SLA Metrics**
  Once embedded in systems and behavior, the SLA provides real-time visibility into whether leads are progressing as expected and converting to pipeline at acceptable rates.
- **You Need to Monitor Execution**
  Use weekly metrics (like Lead-to-Opp Rate and SQL-to-SQO progression) to catch execution gaps, and monthly metrics (like Close Rate and Cycle Time) to track performance and spot systemic issues.
- **SLA Enforcement Is a Muscle, Not a Milestone**
  Most SLA breakdowns aren't strategy failures. Often, they stem from lack of adherence, miscommunication, or weak ownership. CEOs must reinforce this discipline over time.
- **When Red Flags Appear, Look for Patterns**
  A single metric out of range may just be noise, but when multiple red flags appear (declining conversion, rising time in-stage, team friction signals), it might be time to step in.

Chapter 10 Deliverables

By the end of this chapter, your company should have:

- Internal Reporting on SLA Performance
- Board Reporting on SLA Impact
- Sales and Marketing SLA Tracking Meeting
- SLA Red Flags Diagnostic

Why Measuring the SLA Matters

The SLA is how your funnel becomes measurable. More than a coordination tool, it's the mechanism by which Sales and Marketing operate as one system. When executed well, it enforces lead quality, accelerates deal velocity, and gives you a clear, credible view of how your GTM engine converts spend into revenue.

This chapter helps CEOs distinguish between surface-level misalignment and systemic breakdowns and teaches them how to use data to coach cross-functional teams toward accountability and consistency. Done right, the SLA ensures that new money invested to drive leads will net out a return in the end.

10

HOW CEOS MEASURE THE SLA DECISION

THE SLA is how GTM coordination turns into data. Once it is operationalized, CEOs are able to track its impact on pipeline velocity, efficiency, and ROI. Tracking progress on the SLA helps teams catch pipeline problems early, manage accountability better, and report with more accuracy to you, to the board and to future investors at exit.

A successful SLA process yields:

- **Higher lead-to-opportunity conversion rates** by filtering for quality
- **Faster deal velocity** through structured follow-up
- **Improved Rep efficiency** by reducing time spent on low-quality leads
- **Reliable pipeline forecasts** through standardized qualification logic

This chapter covers key metrics, dashboards, and feedback loops CEOs should use to assess SLA health and course-correct when necessary.

INTERNAL REPORTING: IS YOUR SLA WORKING?

Once your SLA is embedded in systems and behavior, the question becomes *Is it improving lead progression and conversion to pipeline?* While sales leaders will manage the day-to-day adherence through progression reports, you need to keep an eye on whether the system at large is producing the results you expect. Use the metrics below to pressure-test the SLA's effectiveness with your commercial leaders. Each metric answers whether a particular conversion point is healthy.

- **Weekly (Execution Check):** ***Are Leads Turning to Opportunities?***
  - **Lead-to-Opp Rate:** Are qualified leads consistently turning into real pipeline?
  - **MQL-to-SQL Rate:** Are MQLs genuinely sales-ready?
  - **SQL-to-SQO Rate:** Are SDRs progressing leads, or is qualification breaking down?
- **Monthly (Performance Check):** ***Are We Converting Efficiently?***
  - **Close Rate by Source:** Are Sales getting "winnable" opportunities from our funded sources?
  - **Cycle Time by Stage:** Are we seeing bottlenecks in certain SLA-defined stages?

These metrics highlight operational adherence and surface where execution gaps, training needs, or SLA definitions may need refining. Keep these on a dashboard, and push your team to act on the signals early.

BOARD REPORTING: HOW THE SLA AFFECTS COMMERCIAL OUTCOMES

Each of the four growth decisions more strongly influences certain commercial board metrics over others. The inbound SLA at the heart of *The Push Framework* has a distinct impact on how efficiently leads convert to pipeline.

When this alignment is working, you'll start to see improvements in conversion rates, faster sales cycles, and, in some cases, an uptick in close rates. These are signs that Marketing and Sales are working as one system, progressing the right leads consistently.

In Figure 35, the metrics in gray are part of the Commercial Board Deck and will be covered in different chapters of the book. are the ones most directly affected when a sound SLA is enforced consistently among teams.

FIGURE 35: Commercial Board Metrics Tied to SLA

Board Metric	Formula	Most Influenced By
ARR Value	Sum of all contracted recurring revenue × 12 months	ICP
New Business Bookings	Total $ of Closed-Won Deals (New Logos Only)	ICP
Logos Won	# of New Logos in Period	ICP
Close Rate	Closed-Won Deals ÷ SQLs	ICP
Deal Size	(Average) Total Closed-Won Revenue ÷ # of Closed-Won Deals or (Median) Middle Value	ICP
Churn Rate	Lost Customers ÷ Total Customers (Start of Period)	ICP
Sales Cycle (Days)	Avg # of Days from First Contact to Close	SLA
Lead-to-Opp Rate	# of Opportunities Created ÷ # of Leads Accepted (SALs) or # of Leads Qualified (MQLs)	SLA
Pipeline Value ($)	Sum of Open Pipeline	Contribution
Pipeline Coverage Ratio (0.0)	Total Pipeline for the Period ÷ Quota for the Period	Contribution
Opportunities Created	# of SQLs or SAOs Created in Period	Contribution

RED FLAGS: WHEN TO REVISIT THE SLA

If you've followed the Push SLA Framework, the core decisions your team made should hold until your ICP changes. Most SLA red flags don't indicate a weak strategy; they indicate weak execution: *inconsistent activity, unclear ownership*, or *lack of oversight*.

Use the metrics below to surface when the SLA needs to be revisited. On their own, each might isolate a short-term execution gap, but when seen together, they can indicate deeper issues in the SLA process.

Metrics Red Flags (seen in combination)

- **Lead-to-Opp Rate declines** quarter over quarter.
- **Time in Stage increases** across key funnel stages.
- **Rejection or Recycle Rates spike** above normal baselines.
- **Close Rate drops**, but lead volume and quality appear steady.

Team Friction Flags

- Competing complaints from Sales and Marketing ("We need more leads" vs. "They're not working the leads we send").
- Funnel stages defined differently across teams.
- SLA performance not tracked or managed with consistency.
- No feedback loop or shared reporting cadence for Sales and Marketing on lead quality in place.

When these red flags appear, the fix isn't always redefining the SLA. It's often about reinforcing adherence, retraining teams, or clarifying ownership. CEOs should coach their sales and marketing leaders to treat SLA enforcement as an ongoing muscle to develop, not a one-time setup.

Now that your team can convert pipeline with consistency, the next question is *Where should that pipeline come from?* Part III covers the Contribution Decision: how to allocate resources from different pipeline sources to drive profitable growth.

CASE STUDY

"We Track That Differently"

The CEO of a $17M fintech company was preparing for the next board meeting. They gathered performance metrics from Sales and Marketing, and found a clear disconnect. Marketing was reporting a high number of leads captured and progressing through the funnel, but Sales' data told a different story, with far fewer leads actually converting to opportunities. Each team used similar, but different, funnel stage names in their reporting, making it difficult for the CEO to reconcile the two reports and find the truth. Lead stages were not standardized and there was no single system acting as the source of truth. Each team used its own reporting to monitor performance and there were no shared dashboards in place to monitor lead progression. The CEO struggled with how to diagnose the delta between high volume of leads and low volume of opportunities, how to accurately project future performance, and what story to tell their investors at the next board meeting.

WHAT THE CEO HEARD FROM THE TEAM

- "Sales says lead quality is poor, but they wait so long to call that the leads have gone cold."
- "Marketing tracks different stages than we do."
- "We report out of different systems, so we track that differently."

WHAT THE CEO SAW IN THE DATA

- Funnel stages defined differently across teams.
- Conflicting lead-to-opportunity conversion rates.
- Data pulled from multiple sources.

SOLUTION

The CEO knew they needed to standardize the commercial KPIs and transform the CRM into a single system of record. To address this, they asked Sales, Marketing, and RevOps to collaborate on standardizing funnel stage names, the exit criteria between each stage, and the attribution rules of engagement between the teams. Before any changes were operationalized, the CEO requested a formal readout to confirm alignment and ensure commitment to the new definitions.

Next, they directed the team to build a shared dashboard to track lead stage progression, time in stage, and conversion rates from lead-to-meeting booked (MQL-to-SQL), and from meeting booked-to-pipeline opened (SQL-to-SQO). They also instituted a weekly performance review between Sales and Marketing and committed to joining those meetings until progress gained traction.

By creating a common language, aligning on a single source of truth, and reinforcing cross-functional accountability, the team built the muscle to discuss and diagnose lead quality together. By the next board meeting, all three leaders could present a unified commercial narrative and prove progress with data.

PART III

THE CONTRIBUTION DECISION

EXECUTIVE SUMMARY 11

THE CONTRIBUTION DECISION DEFINED

Key Takeaways

- **The Contribution Model Is Your Bookings Plan**
  It cascades the bookings target down into pipeline goals, then further down into funnel-specific goals. By isolating these variables, you give each team clear activity-based levers they can monitor and improve in real time.
- ***The Push Framework* Goes Beyond Traditional Contribution Modeling**
  Standard models stop at funnel math. *The Push Framework* uses a collaborative workshop format to translate bookings targets to owned activity goals. It identifies growth levers the team can use to deliver on those goals and establishes a method for real-time performance tracking.
- **The CEO Must Participate to Surface Growth Levers**
  When the CEO participates, strategic growth levers can surface that can shape the company's priorities for the long-term. Without the CEO in the room, these levers are more likely to be missed, glossed over, or ignored as "someone else's problem."
- **CFO Oversight**
  When the CFO helps build the model in the room, they can bring that context to the governance later on. Positioning the CFO to

oversee pacing to the plan frees you up to focus on OKRs and other strategic endeavors.

Why the Contribution Decision Matters

For the CEO, the Contribution Decision is about more than just modeling. It's your opportunity to pressure-test whether your GTM engine can realistically deliver the pipeline and bookings needed to achieve your revenue targets. It breaks down your bookings target into pipeline targets, by segment, and then further cascades them down into logo-specific activity goals your teams can track on a week-by-week basis.

The workshop format forces clarity, surfaces strategic growth levers, and drives functional alignment on what needs to happen and who's responsible for delivering it. It also gives you and the CFO early visibility of execution risk. Instead of waiting until Q4 to find out you're off pace, you'll see and can address performance issues in real time as one team. In *The Push Framework*, your CFO is positioned to become your governance arm, pacing to the plan with the group. By participating in the modeling conversation, they gain the context needed to hold the team accountable after the fact.

You can't build a credible contribution plan until you've made your ICP and SLA Decisions. To reach this point, your team had to align first with which customer segments to target and agree on the stages your prospects will go through to graduate from lead to pipeline. With both of those decisions made, your company now has the infrastructure and the shared language needed to model future growth as one commercial unit. That's a major milestone. It means your team is ready to build a plan they can envision, own, and deliver together.

Ultimately, the Contribution Model signals GTM maturity and control. It enables you to tell a data-backed growth story to your teams, your board, and eventually your next buyer at exit.

11

THE CONTRIBUTION DECISION DEFINED

THE CONTRIBUTION DECISION answers the question *How, and how much, will each function contribute to our bookings target?* Bookings refers to the total value of new and expansion contracts your team must sign this year to stay on track for long-term revenue growth. While revenue is recognized over time, bookings are what GTM teams execute against in real time.

Your investor probably set a revenue CAGR target as part of the investment thesis. This growth rate defines what your business must deliver annually in recognized revenue for the investor to achieve their return over a three- to five-year hold.

A revenue target, however, is the outcome, not the plan. To make it actionable, you need to break it down into targets your team can execute against week after week, month after month, year after year.

This starts with bookings. Each year, the revenue target implies a bookings requirement. To reach that target, it must be broken down into pipeline targets and then further into logo- activity targets that your teams can manage to weekly and monthly. That's the waterfall (see Figure 36).

FIGURE 36: Revenue Waterfall

Level	Metric	What It Represents	Owner
REVENUE-BASED	CAGR Target	Growth rate required to achieve investor returns (set in the investment thesis)	CEO
	Revenue (ARR)	Annual recognized revenue implied by the CAGR	CEO
	Bookings	Annual contract value required to hit the revenue target	GTM Team
	Pipeline	Estimated bookings value of opportunities in the sales process.	GTM Team
ACTIVITY-BASED	Opportunities	Prospects actively in the sales process	GTM Team
	Meetings	Prospects who are interested in meeting with a sales representative	GTM Team
	Leads	Prospects who have expressed interest but are not yet in the sales process	GTM Team

That translation, from bookings dollars to logo-activity targets, is the job of the Contribution Model. In the Push Contribution Framework, the model is created in a workshop with your team. In that workshop, you start with the bookings target and engage your team to build a bottom-up plan that tests whether your current funnel performance, Sales capacity, and Marketing output can deliver it. Your job as CEO is to lead this strategic exercise, pressure-test your team's assumptions, and listen for growth levers that have the potential to move the needle for the business.

In the workshop, your team will model contribution by answering four key questions:

- *How much pipeline do we need (by segment and by team)?*
- *Are today's conversion rates, deal sizes, and cycle times enough to generate that pipeline?*
- *Can the teams deliver their share of pipeline with current headcount and budgets?*
- *If we're short, where do we invest, reallocate, or improve?*

The model cascades the bookings target into pipeline goals, then further into funnel-level inputs: *lead volume, meetings held, conversion rates, rep productivity,* and *program spend*. By isolating these variables, you give each team clear performance targets they can monitor and improve in real time. The Contribution Model becomes a bookings plan you and the team can track to every week or month.

If the model doesn't add up, then you've surfaced the shortfall early, when you still have time to course-correct. Modeling like this is how you avoid missing your number in Q4 and having to explain it in hindsight.

A key benefit of the Contribution Model is that it gives you something you and the team can react to in real time to stay on pace to hit the revenue targets. Instead of hoping things will come together at the end of the quarter, you build a system that can flag where you're off track and what needs to improve, weeks or months in advance.

CONTRIBUTION VS. ATTRIBUTION

Contribution and attribution are not the same thing. Contribution assigns ownership for revenue targets from different sources, based on what each must deliver to hit the company's overall bookings target.

Typical Contribution sources include:

- Marketing for inbound
- Sales or Marketing for outbound
- Sales or Partner for partners
- Marketing or Product for self-serve

Sometimes called waterfall metrics, funnel math, or demand modeling, Contribution informs strategic planning and resource allocation.

Attribution (the reporting you set up in the previous SLA chapters) refers to the ROI tracking specific to lead-generating channels or sources, typically using first-touch (initial engagement), last-touch (final engagement leading to conversion), or multi-touch (shared credit across multiple interactions) models. Attribution tracking is one layer deeper than Contribution. It helps you understand which tactics are generating demand, but it doesn't tell you whether the team managing those tactics is set up to deliver their target (see Figure 37).

Attribution rolls up to Contribution. It explains where leads come from while Contribution defines who owns the number.

RULE OF 40 AFFECTS YOUR CONTRIBUTION DECISION

For PE-backed companies, scaling to $100M achieving growth alone isn't enough. Many investors set a Rule of X standard for their companies to meet (commonly a Rule of 40 or Rule of 50). This metric is calculated by adding your annual revenue growth rate to your EBITDA margin. It is used by investors to assess whether the company is scaling in a capital-efficient way.

FIGURE 37: Contribution vs. Attribution

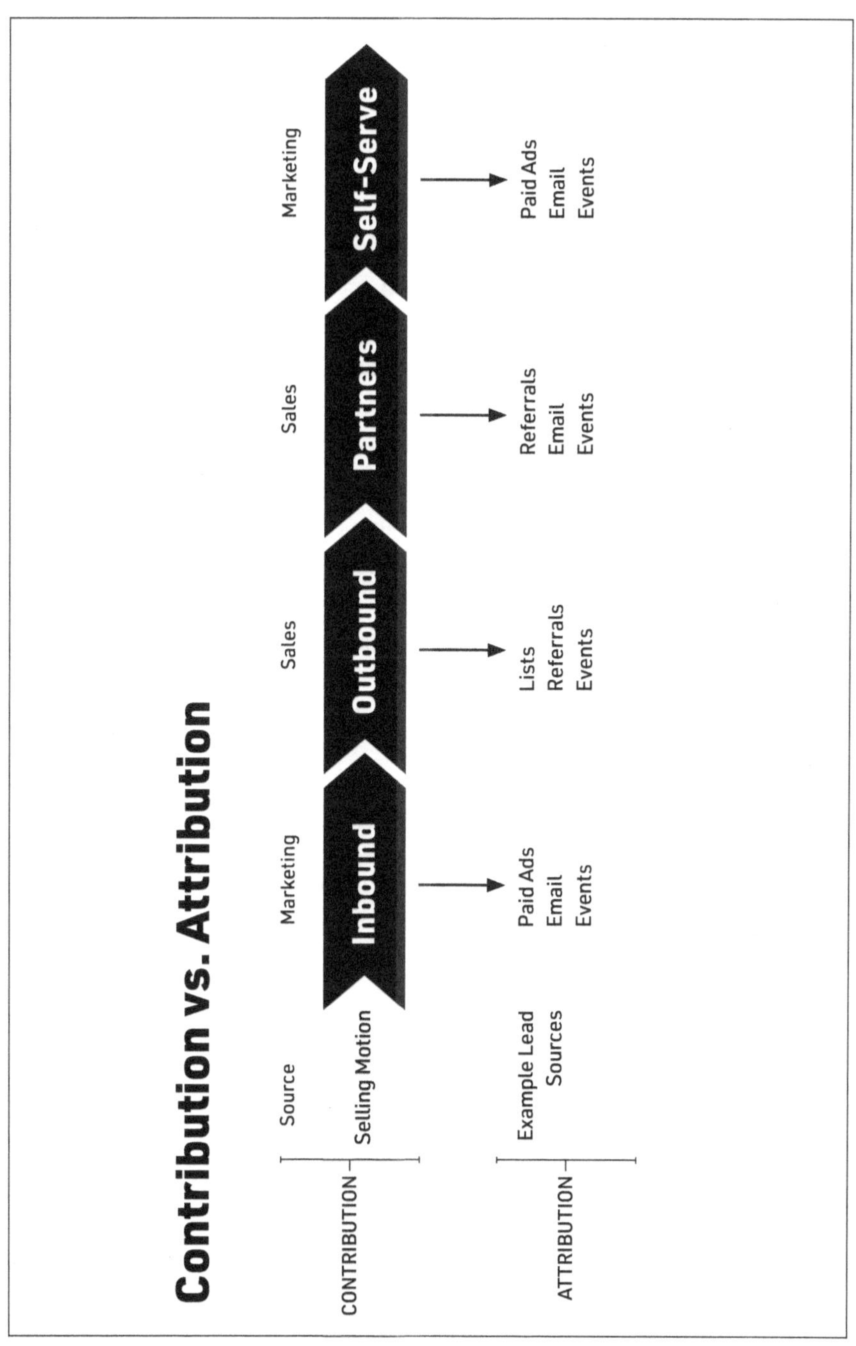

Here is a Rule of 40 example. If your company has:

- Annual Revenue Growth: 32%
- EBITDA Margin: 12%

Then your Rule of X profile would be 44 (32 + 12)

Some investors prefer a growth-weighted Rule of 40 profile, especially for early-growth stage companies still capturing market share. Others expect you to drive improvements in margin discipline year-over-year. As CEO, you need to understand where your investors stand.

This understanding will directly influence the resource trade-offs you make during the Contribution Workshop: whether to push for headcount, increase program spend, or trim in favor of efficiency. It also sets you up for the OKR Decision coming in Part IV, where you'll align the company around the near-term activities that will set you on the path to achieve your Exit Targets.

If you haven't had this conversation yet, now is the time to ask your investors: *Do you want Rule of X performance to come from topline growth, margin expansion, or a balanced mix?*

WHAT MAKES THE PUSH CONTRIBUTION FRAMEWORK DIFFERENT

Most Contribution Models stop at assigning a number. They define how much revenue or pipeline each team needs to generate, but leave execution disconnected among the teams.

The Push Contribution Framework links the bookings model directly to functional execution and installs a clear tracking owner to keep teams accountable throughout the year.

In the following chapters about contribution, you'll learn how to make the Contribution Decision, align GTM teams with it, and operationalize it in four steps:

1. **Contribution Workshop:** Facilitated by the CEO or a neutral third-party facilitator, the workshop aligns functional leaders

with bookings targets and defines leads, opportunities, deals, and conversion rates by source (inbound, outbound, partners, account management) for key ICP segments (from Part I).

2. **Quota Setting and Territory Planning:** Sales will plan capacity, territories, and quotas based on the contribution expectations from the model, informed by the ICP segments and the number of scored accounts available (from Part I).
3. **Full-Funnel Campaign Planning:** Marketing will take their pipeline, lead, and conversion targets from the model and build a full-funnel campaign plan rooted in the ICP definition (from Part I) and leveraging the SLA Decision (from Part II) for efficiency.
4. **Model Tracking Meetings:** After the session, the CFO becomes the plan's governance owner, running weekly or monthly tracking reviews to monitor pacing, flag execution risk, and hold teams accountable for their share of the bookings plan. The CFO ensures the model stays connected to the commitments made to the board.

Unlike standard models, the Push Contribution Framework creates a shared bookings plan between Sales and *all teams* who source pipeline. It reinforces that alignment by setting up quotas and campaign plans on shared pipeline targets and installs your CFO as your proxy to govern progress to those shared targets regularly.

WHY THE CONTRIBUTION DECISION COMES THIRD

The work you've done so far in the Push Order of Operations has been leading you to this point. You cannot credibly set contribution targets without first aligning with the customer segments you need to set bookings targets against (see Part I: ICP Decision) or without the funnel stages you plan to set logo-level goals against (see Part II: SLA Decision). You can only build a realistic, bottom- up Contribution Model once your teams share the same understanding of these two components.

One of the key differentiators of the Push Contribution Framework is its workshop format. When Contribution is modeled collaboratively in a workshop, instead of by one team member in a silo, it often reveals not just whether your team can hit the number, but what's missing to hit the number.

GROWTH LEVERS

A well-facilitated Contribution Workshop puts you and your CFO in the same room with your commercial leaders to pressure-test assumptions and build the plan together. In this setting, strategic growth levers emerge naturally, many of which are either missed when modeling happens in a silo (even by a capable GTM leader) or ignored as "someone else's problem" when the CEO isn't in the room.

These growth levers can look like a need for:

- A down-market product to gain speed to revenue
- A new contribution source, like partners, to supplement lead volume
- A pricing study to increase deal size

The growth levers that surface from this discussion often extend beyond the reasonable remit of the commercial team and are actually company-level priorities. For example, a need for a down-market product requires tight alignment with Product and Engineering. A partner strategy may require support from Enablement, Legal, and Finance. These are not isolated sales or marketing initiatives; they're cross-functional investments that must be prioritized, planned, and tracked at the executive level.

Surfacing these types of growth levers is why Contribution Decision is a prerequisite to the OKR Decision in Part IV. That final growth decision is where you'll decide what the company will align around, resource, and execute in terms of long-term priorities.

CEO ROLE

Making and managing a cohesive Contribution Model is the hallmark of a mature, strategic go-to-market organization. It demonstrates alignment through shared goals among Sales, Marketing, Customer Success, and others. This model gives you a data-backed way to explain or defend the company's plan to hit bookings and installs the infrastructure to help your teams respond quickly to progress on that plan in real time.

For CEOs, the Contribution Model offers clear visibility of the goals the company plans to achieve leading up to the topline bookings number. Articulating this clearly to the board reinforces your strategic control, forecast discipline, and accountability for revenue performance.

To lead effectively through this stage, the CEO must:

- **Identify Growth Levers:** Actively listen for strategic initiatives that emerge during the workshop, such as pricing adjustments, new market entry, or channel expansion. These types of levers can be needle-movers. They have the potential to drive significant growth over the next several years.
- **Align with the Investment Thesis:** Use the CAGR target, Rule of X, and Value Creation Plan as your directional compass. These provide clues about which direction the model needs to take for a successful exit to the next round of investment.
- **Empower the CFO:** Position the CFO as the governance owner of the Contribution Model, not just the financial monitor. Their role is to track pacing, flag risk, and drive accountability among the different teams. For some CFOs, this will also be a learning opportunity to deepen their understanding of how GTM activities translate into financial outcomes.

As CEO, your participation is critical to driving an investor-aligned Contribution Model, but participation doesn't have to mean facilitation.

WHEN TO OUTSOURCE

The Contribution Workshop is one of the few GTM planning moments where it's almost always better to have a strong facilitator than try to wing it. This is not just a modeling exercise; it's a candid conversation where leaders are asked to expose what they know, what they can deliver, and what they need from others to commit. Done well, the session tightens alignment and ownership. Done poorly, it can surface resentment, misalignment, or defensive behavior that can set your execution back.

If you anticipate tension between teams or if your leaders haven't had this kind of structured conversation before, then investing in a neutral, SaaS-savvy facilitator is often the better path.

In Chapter 12, you'll find the workshop discussion guide to help you lead this session effectively yourself, but fair warning: This is often *the most* sensitive conversation your commercial leaders will engage in. It benefits from expert handling and care.

Use the two scenarios below to determine which kind of facilitation partner is right for your circumstance.

Option 1: Company Has Product-Market Fit

If your company has product-market fit (confirmed during the ICP Decision) and a capable GTM leadership team in place, then the goal is straightforward: to align on go-forward growth levers and shared execution. In this scenario, you need a skilled facilitator who can:

- Manage internal dynamics
- Probe constructively for growth levers
- Help the team arrive at realistic, cross-functional targets

The right partner is typically a growth advisor with deep SaaS experience in leading strategic conversations. These engagements are short (typically one day), modest in cost ($), and high in impact. If your investor has Operating Partners or an in-house advisory team, start there. They may be able to do this for you at no charge.

Option 2: Company Has Lost Product-Market Fit

Less common but more consequential, this option applies when your company no longer has clear product-market fit: a reality that may be discovered later in the hold period. Here, the need goes beyond facilitation. You'll require a strategic partner who can conduct:

- Market research
- Segment viability analysis
- Competitive positioning reviews
- Pricing and packaging diagnostics

This is typically a two- to three-month engagement led by a strategic consulting firm with sector-specific expertise. Expect a significant investment ($$$$), from which you get a detailed and defensible plan that could reshape your go-to-market strategy entirely. For companies in this position, this will be more than a Contribution Model. It is a defining decision that determines your ability to rebound, reposition, or exit successfully.

Whether you choose to lead the workshop yourself or bring in expert support, this is not a conversation to take lightly. For CEOs, this is the defensible version of your growth story, backed with data, informed by the experts on your team, and held accountable by your CFO.

Regardless of whether you facilitate the workshop yourself or outsource it, Chapter 12 will walk you through how to play the lead role in making the Contribution Decision.

CASE STUDY

A Great Math Exercise, But An Unrealistic Plan

The CEO and CFO of a $50M edtech company worked with investors on the annual operating plan for the first year of their investment. They targeted 20% YoY ARR growth based on two inputs: Average deal size had increased in the prior year, and Sales planned to add two new Reps to help bring in more deals. To preserve margin, they held the Marketing budget flat.

The numbers made sense and the calculations were sound, but the model was not stress-tested. It lacked the bottom-up assumptions about Sales and Marketing performance needed to confirm that the model was realistic. By the end of the first quarter, YoY growth had slowed; by the second quarter, the team missed plan for the first time. The CEO was at a loss and looked to the sales leader to explain the miss.

WHAT THE CEO HEARD FROM THE TEAM

- "We're not getting enough qualified pipeline."
- "We aren't closing big enough accounts to hit that deal size."
- "The reps are not cold-calling."

WHAT THE CEO SAW IN THE DATA

- Lead volume nearly all sourced by inbound
- Pipeline stalled and below target
- Actual deal sizes below average

SOLUTION

Without a clear diagnosis of what was going wrong, the CEO paused and reconvened the cross-functional commercial team to isolate the variables in a collaborative Contribution Workshop. The CFO brought the topline target and together, the team rebuilt the bottom-up model based on the latest performance for each funnel stage. Using this updated model, they were able to identify three gaps that were stalling pipeline and needed to close:

- **Marketing** couldn't scale qualified lead volume without additional budget, due to rising CAC from increased competition.
- **Sales** was relying almost entirely on inbound leads and not running outbound plays to generate new incremental pipeline.
- **Average deal size** was inflated by a few large accounts from the prior year that did not reflect the typical customer.

With these gaps exposed, the team could react. The CFO reset the model using the median deal size, which significantly increased the number of leads and opportunities needed to hit the plan. To close the gap, Sales agreed to take on a bookings target tied to outbound Rep activity, and the CEO approved a budget increase for Marketing to support the rest. The team agreed to review funnel KPIs weekly with the CFO, creating a regular cadence to track progress and course-correct misses in real time.

The revised plan gave the CEO, CFO, and GTM leaders a clear line of sight into what had to happen, and who owned what, to get back on track. The CEO was able to present a data-backed narrative to the board, explaining the root cause of the miss and the specific actions underway to remediate. Within three weeks, pipeline began to recover. Within three months, bookings followed. By the end of the following quarter, the team had stabilized and regained momentum.

EXECUTIVE SUMMARY 12

HOW CEOS MAKE THE CONTRIBUTION DECISION

Key Takeaways

- **This is a Litmus Test for Your Leadership Team**
  This can be one of the most revealing conversations you'll lead as a CEO, so pay attention to how your leaders show up. Do they understand their role in driving growth, are they realistic in evaluating performance, are they collaborative?
- **No Single Function Can Speak for the Others**
  When Contribution Models are built in isolation by one person, they often focus on what has to be generated rather than what has to be true to generate it. This marks the difference between a math exercise and a bookings plan.
- **Don't Expect an Easy Conversation**
  This is supposed to be a vulnerable discussion. Leaders must expose what they can commit to and what they need from other leaders to be successful. When expertly facilitated, it builds alignment and reveals strategic growth levers. When mishandled, it breeds tension and stalls progress.
- **Growth Levers from the Contribution Workshop Fuel OKRs**
  This discussion can surface some of your company's most powerful growth levers, such as pricing changes, market expansion shifts, or new selling motions. For that reason, the

Contribution Decision comes just before the final Push Decision (the OKR Decision, Part IV), where you'll consider operationalizing some of these growth levers as your company priorities.

Chapter 12 Deliverables

By the end of this chapter, your team will have:

- A Bottom-Up Contribution Model
- A Resource Plan Based on Contribution Goals

Why Making the Contribution Decision Matters

The Contribution Workshop is one of the most important strategic discussions you'll have with your team. The model that the team puts together in the room will answer how you plan to hit your bookings target this year as one team. Too often, growth targets are accepted without a clear, shared understanding of what has to happen stage-by-stage or week-by-week to achieve them. This chapter helps your team scenario-plan what has to be true to hit those targets.

What makes Contribution Modeling different in *The Push Framework* is how it's made: not in isolation like a math exercise, but in the open with all of your commercial leaders at the table. This collaborative planning session turns the bookings target in a shared goal for the team. The model that comes from this workshop becomes your bookings plan for the year: a living artifact that can be groomed weekly or monthly in reaction to the team's performance.

For CEOs, the Contribution Model unlocks several forms of leverage. First, it surfaces the tradeoffs required to achieve your bookings target. That can look like investing more in Marketing, making needed improvements in mid-funnel conversion rates, or rebalancing contribution between inbound and outbound.

Second, it clarifies who owns what. When conversion rates are off, the team doesn't just report the miss; they understand what the rate needs to be to hit plan and that they must react to that miss with some kind of improvement.

Third, it positions the CFO to take on a new role: not just as financial monitor, but as your proxy. With a strong model in place and the CFO leading the tracking meeting, the CEO is free to focus elsewhere, knowing the plan is in good hands.

12

HOW CEOS MAKE THE CONTRIBUTION DECISION

DURATION: 1 DAY FOR DECISION (DAY 32)

IN THE PUSH FRAMEWORK, teams make the Contribution Decision by live-modeling contribution in a cross-functional workshop designed to scenario-plan ideas using data assumptions to validate their growth plans.

A Contribution Model sets bottom-up projections on leads, opportunities, and deals by applying assumed conversion rates at each stage of the funnel in each planned selling motion (inbound, outbound, partner, self-serve, expansion). Combining strategic conversations with real-time data in this way helps leaders ground their plans in practical, measurable outcomes.

This conversation often requires a neutral party capable of managing tension and uncovering growth opportunities to facilitate (typically the CEO, CFO, or a third-party advisor). GTM leaders are generally not a good choice as facilitators because they often have conflicting interests that can turn the decision-making exercise into a tense debate.

This can be one of the most revealing conversations you'll lead as a CEO, so pay attention to how your team shows up.

- *How clearly does each leader understand their role in driving growth?*
- *How realistically do they evaluate their team's performance?*
- *How collaboratively are they willing to plan?*

This discussion can also surface some of your company's most powerful growth levers. Many of these insights could fuel your next phase of growth. For that reason, the Contribution Decision comes just before the final growth decision (see Part IV: OKR Decision), where you'll consider prioritizing some of these growth levers as your company objectives.

When following the Push Contribution Workshop facilitation guide, you'll lead the team through a structured discussion that aligns with what must be true to hit the plan. Along the way, you'll answer questions like:

- *How many logos, and much in bookings, can your team realistically commit to?*
- *Is average deal size a realistic input, or should we switch to median?*
- *What conversion metric must improve (and who owns it) to reach our goals?*
- *Is this model realistic; where do we see risk?*
- *Do we have enough Marketing budget or Sales headcount to support the plan?*

While the conversation reveals growth levers and constraints, the answers are codified directly into the model. You'll define measurable targets for each source (inbound, outbound, partners, PLG/self-serve) and segment (aligned to your ICP definition), including the following.

CONTRIBUTION MODEL OUTPUTS

- Bookings Target
- Logo Targets
- Conversion Rates at key funnel stages:
  - Lead to MQL
  - MQL to SQL

- SQL to Opportunity
- Opportunity to Win (Win Rate)

- Lead Volumes required to support funnel targets
- Pipeline Targets
- Marketing Budget required to meet plan commitments
- Rep or BDR Headcount required to connect net-new outbound prospects and qualify inbound leads

The outcome is a bottom-up, cross-functionally owned Contribution Model: your year-ahead bookings plan, anchored in data and built to be governed through KPI tracking and weekly operating cadences.

NO ONE FUNCTION CAN SPEAK FOR THE OTHERS

Not all Contribution Models are created equal. Traditional models, often built in isolation by the CFO or CRO, tend to focus too narrowly on inbound lead volume and closed deals. When developed in a silo, these models become little more than a math exercise disconnected from day-to-day execution and blind to functional constraints. In this approach, the Contribution Model is treated as a read-out to answer the question, *How many leads do we need to hit our number?* rather than a coordinated plan for where teams plan to source those leads and what has to be true to convert them to pipeline and achieve the company's target.

No single function, not even the CFO or CRO, can speak for the entire GTM engine. That's why this decision is made collaboratively in a workshop setting. When leaders discuss, debate, and scenario-plan their assumptions, the Contribution Model shifts from simply a spreadsheet to a playbook that is grounded in reality; one that is trackable through clear KPIs over time.

THE CFO BECOMES THE CEO PROXY

When the leadership team commits to Contribution targets with the CFO in the room, the CEO effectively activates the CFO's role as the guardian of the bookings plan.

For many CFOs, participating in the Contribution Workshop unlocks a shift from understanding the math behind the revenue to understanding the interlocks behind how a GTM team generates that revenue. That context elevates their ability to track progress with the team after the fact and equips them better to help you articulate the story behind the numbers in the boardroom and at exit.

Investors don't expect perfection, but they do expect fluency, command, and responsiveness. They want to know that the CEO and CFO are aligned; the team is operating from a shared model; and when gaps emerge, there's a mechanism in place to address them with urgency. This governance setup delivers on that.

Positioning the CFO this way is a strategic differentiator. Rather than leaving Sales, Marketing, and Customer Success to manage their own parts of the plan independently, the CFO becomes the proxy for the CEO by overseeing execution of the model through regular team reviews. In this cadence, the CFO can act as an extension of the CEO, ensuring that progress continues to align with executive and board priorities.

This setup creates leverage for the CEO. With the CFO running point on weekly reviews, the CEO can focus on steering strategic direction, knowing that performance against the plan is being tracked appropriately.

COMMON CEO MISTAKE: EXPECTING AN EASY CONVERSATION

This is not supposed to be an easy conversation. When this conversation is done right, the leaders in the room will be answering sensitive questions like *Can you hit this target?* or *What will it take to improve this conversion rate?* These kinds of questions can put leaders on the defensive and create a greater rift on teams if not handled well.

If tensions already exist between the sales and marketing leaders, don't assume you can power through it. A neutral facilitator with expertise in SaaS growth can make or break your ability to craft a bookings plan the team will commit to. The facilitation guide that follows will help you lead the conversation, but if you sense the risk of escalating conflict or misalignment, bring in expert facilitation. It's a small investment to protect a decision that will define your go-to-market performance for the year.

STEP 10: CONTRIBUTION WORKSHOP

Owner: *CEO,* **Duration:** *4–8 Hours (Day 69)*

Few discussions can stress-test your growth strategy more effectively than the Contribution Workshop. Its success depends on facilitating the session effectively with the right stakeholders.

Participants and Roles

- **CEO (Facilitator):** Leads the discussion, ensures strategic alignment, challenges assumptions, and facilitates constructive debate on realistic targets and growth levers.
- **CFO (Model Preparation and Validation):** Prepares the Contribution Model with initial assumptions and ensures real-time data modeling and validates assumptions during the workshop.
- **Heads of Sales, Marketing, Customer Success (Commercial Leadership Team):** Provide insights, debate, and commitment to realistic targets for their respective functions.
- **Heads of BDR, Channel Partnerships, Demand Generation, Account Management, and RevOps (Supporting Validation):** Join as available to provide a realistic point of view, validate assumptions about funnel performance, and ensure accurate commitments.

Decisions to Make

- **Bookings Targets:** What's the bookings target by selling motion and ICP segment?
- **Pipeline Targets:** How much pipeline do we want to convert to cushion quotas?
- **Logo Targets:** How many logos are needed to hit the plan?
- **Conversion Rate Goals:** What are the required conversion rates by stage and source?
- **Achievability:** Are volume and conversion assumptions realistic?

- **Resource Needs:** What Marketing spend and BDR headcount are required?
- **Gaps & Risks:** Where are the pressure points or unrealistic assumptions?

FIGURE 38: Contribution Workshop Agenda

Duration	Agenda	Owner	Attendees
Prep	Prep the Contribution Model Template: Prepare the model template to use in the workshop. Include Bookings Target, Deal Size, Average Sales Cycle, Historical or Best-Guess by Segment	CFO	Leaders of: • Sales • Marketing • Customer Success • BDR • Demand Gen • Partner
15 min.	**Kickoff & Objectives:** Workshop purpose, topline target review, expectations for collaboration	CEO	
15 min.	**Template Introduction:** Introduce structure, segments, baseline assumptions	CFO	
30 min.	**Set Bookings Targets by Source (First Segment):** Source definitions, past performance, achievable targets, logo conversion	CEO, Facilitator	
90 min.	**Model the Funnel from the Bottom Up:** Funnel stages, conversion rates, volume checks, owner assignments, scenario planning		
30 min.	**Resource Planning:** Marketing budget (CPL-based), BDR headcount (inbound/outbound), feasibility review		
15 min.	**Finalize Segment Model:** Volume reasonability, owner confirmation, risk identification		
60+ min.	**Repeat for Additional Segments:** Above flow for remaining ICP segments		
15 min.	**Wrap-Up & Next Steps:** Summarize decisions, assign follow-ups, confirm KPI tracking cadence		

How-To Model Contribution

STEP 1: PREP THE CONTRIBUTION MODEL (CFO-LED, BEFORE THE WORKSHOP)

Ask the CFO to build a Contribution Model template that can support a monthly bookings target over the next 24 months (to accommodate longer sales cycles). They will create this template for each of the key segments aligned to the ICP definitions from Part I (e.g., NAM, EMEA, APAC or SMB, MM, ENT). The models should include baseline assumptions for:

1. Bookings targets by segment
2. Pipeline targets by segments (generally lands between 2x–4x of bookings target)
3. Average or median deal size
4. Average sales cycle
5. Historical conversion rate placeholders or best-guess rates

If you don't have reliable or historical funnel conversion rates to start with, then it's okay to use best-guess estimates. This model is a starting point. You'll refine it regularly with actuals through the governance meetings that follow.

Plan to workshop one ICP segment at a time.

STEP 2: SET BOOKINGS TARGETS BY SELLING MOTION

Introduce the selling motions your company plans to use for demand generation: inbound, outbound, partner, self-serve/PLG, expansion. For the purposes of this book, the following examples will map to the following teams.

- *Inbound* = Marketing Team
- *Outbound* = Sales Team
- *Partner* = Sales Team
- *Self-Serve/PLG* = Marketing Team
- *Expansion* = Customer Success Team

- For each:
    a. Ask, *Based on past performance and planned changes, what bookings target can your team commit to?*
    b. Convert bookings to logo targets (by dividing by the average or median deal size).
    c. Compare targets to historical performance. Ask, *Is this achievable?*
    d. Document bookings and logo targets by source for the first segment.

You might revisit these decisions later in the workshop as you scenario-plan to test assumptions.

STEP 3: BUILD THE FUNNEL GOALS FROM THE BOTTOM UP

1. Using the logo target from Step 2, model up the funnel to calculate what's required at each stage. Example for Inbound:

    Logo Wins → Opportunities → SQLs → MQLs → Leads

2. Repeat this approach for the rest of the channels as appropriate.
3. Scenario-plan different conversion rates to gut-check what the rates need to be to achieve the logo target for that source. As you enter the conversion rates, calculate the resulting volumes and use them as the sanity check.
    Ask:
    a. *Is this volume achievable? Is it enough?*
    b. *If not, what must change to improve this metric?*
    c. *Who on your team will own the improvement?*
4. Document the final conversion rates by source for the first segment.

You might revisit these decisions again after the next step.

STEP 4: RESOURCE PLAN

Reality-check whether you have enough resources to support the plan.

1. **Marketing Budget:** Calculate the program spend required to generate the necessary lead volume. Use a *blended* Cost Per Lead (CPL) rather than last-click CPL to reflect the true cost of multi-touch marketing.

   Blended CPL formula:

   Total Marketing Spend ÷ Total Leads Generated
   (from all sources, for the past 6 weeks)

   A blended CPL accounts for all marketing-sourced leads captured in a certain time period regardless of channel. It includes direct, referral, and organic leads. Using this CPL accounts for the halo effect of brand, content, SEO, and other activities that drive leads but may not show up in attribution reporting. With the blended CPL, you can then identify the needed program spend for your marketing programs.

   Estimate Program Spend:

   Target Lead Count x Blended Cost Per Lead (CPL) =
   Required Program Spend

2. **BDR Headcount Calculation:** Estimate the number of Reps needed to handle the lead and outreach volumes.

   Outbound BDRs = Total Connects Required
   (i.e. spoke with prospect) ÷ **Connects per BDR per Month**

Inbound BDRs = Total Inbound Leads ÷ Qualified Leads per BDR per Month

Hybrid Total = Outbound BDRs + Inbound BDRs

If the spend or headcount required seems excessive, then you need to revisit the earlier decisions. Follow this sequence:

1. **Review funnel metrics:** Are conversion assumptions too conservative?
2. **Identify improvement levers:** Where could performance be optimized (e.g., conversion rates from MQL to SQL)?
3. **Reallocate bookings mix:** Shift contribution to a more efficient source (e.g., from inbound to partner).

STEP 5: FINALIZE AND REPEAT THIS MODELING FOR THE REMAINING SEGMENTS

With funnel stage targets and resource requirements in place, it's time to pressure-test the full model and confirm ownership throughout the team.

1. **Review the Full Funnel For Each Selling Motion**
   a. Confirm that stage volume goals feel achievable given current performance.
   b. Adjust bookings allocation among sources as needed for balance.
2. **Confirm Ownership and Risks**
   a. Identify any funnel stage where conversion rates must improve.
   b. Assign clear owners for each performance lever (e.g., *Who will own increasing SQL-to-Opportunity from 30% to 40%?*).
   c. Flag known risks or dependencies (e.g., hiring timeline, tooling, enablement needs).

Once this segment is finalized, repeat the process for the next segment. When all segments are complete, you'll have a full, cross-functional, bottom-up bookings plan ready to execute in the next chapter with sales quotas, territories, and marketing campaign plans.

EXECUTIVE SUMMARY 13

HOW CEOS EXECUTE THE CONTRIBUTION DECISION

Key Takeaways

- **Aligning Quotas with Campaign Plans is a Maturity Milestone**
  In *The Push Framework*, both Sales and Marketing work toward the same pipeline targets with quotas and campaigns. In this way, marketing sources the pipeline and Sales converts it. This alignment is a key sign of GTM maturity and unlocks predictable growth.
- **Sales Governance is a Risk**
  Without clear visibility into Rep pacing and territory performance, bookings gaps surface too late. CEOs don't need to run Sales governance, but they do need to confirm it's in place. It's easy to assume Sales is managing execution, but many teams lack the structure to catch risks early.
- **Marketing Can Own a Bookings Target**
  Campaigns that stop at lead generation won't deliver bookings. When campaigns support both demand generation and sales enablement programs, Marketing has enough influence to take on a marketing-sourced bookings target (making them true partners in revenue).
- **A Campaign Theme Unlocks Long-Term Messaging**
  To support the full buyer journey from research to renewal, SaaS campaigns generally need to run for six to 12 months or more. A

strong campaign theme creates consistent messaging throughout the funnel, which enables long-term planning.

- **CFO Tracking Turns the Contribution Model from a Forecast to a Plan**
  Governance is what turns your bookings model into an execution plan. By leading regular tracking reviews, the CFO becomes your proxy by monitoring performance, surfacing gaps, and facilitating real-time adjustments.

Chapter 13 Deliverables

By the end of this chapter, your team will have:

- Territories and Quotas
- Marketing Campaign Plan
- CFO-Led Contribution Tracking

Why Executing the Contribution Decision Matters

No single team achieves the bookings target alone. This chapter embeds the Contribution Model, your team's shared bookings plan, into Sales and Marketing's day-to-day activities and installs the governance cadence to keep it all on track.

The work of this chapter puts the first three foundational decisions into action:

- **The ICP Decision** aligned your team on which segments to pursue.
- **The SLA Decision** defined how leads convert to pipeline.
- **The Contribution Decision** quantified the pipeline and bookings target by source that Sales and Marketing would share.

For CEOs, the work of this chapter gives you visibility into what's driving (or blocking) pipeline; confidence that teams are executing against the same plan; and a governance mechanism that enables the CFO to keep pace, performance, and board expectations in sync.

13

HOW CEOS EXECUTE THE CONTRIBUTION DECISION

DURATION: 30 DAYS FOR EXECUTION (DAY 70–100)

THIS CHAPTER puts the bookings plan you made in Chapter 12 into action. Executing the Contribution Model means using what came out of that workshop to inform some of your everyday commercial practices. Because this model sets pipeline and in-funnel conversion rate goals, there are a lot of places where the model can be embedded to direct the activities of the commercial team. This chapter focuses on the three most critical activities that must be in place, *and informed by the Contribution Model*, to hit your bookings plan. Over the next 30 days, your sales leader, marketing leader, and CFO will execute on the model in these ways:

- Sales will use it to set quotas and design territories.
- Marketing will use the model to inform their campaign plan.
- CFO will establish recurring tracking meetings with the team.

By the end of this chapter, you should have the Contribution Model embedded in these sales and marketing practices, as well as a recurring governance cadence established by the CFO to monitor and track performance to the model goals.

CEO ROLE

You are empowering the CFO to step in as your proxy and govern progress against the model targets, so the lift for the CEO in this execution phase is relatively light. As CEO, your job during execution is to ensure that the model's pipeline targets are set as sales quotas targets and marketing campaign targets as described in the next two steps. If you are following the 100-Day Plan schedule, you will notice that all three of the execution steps will run in parallel.

We'll start with Sales.

STEP 11: TERRITORIES AND QUOTAS

Owner: *Sales Leader,* **Duration:** *14 Days (Days 70–84)*

Territory planning divides your market into manageable segments to balance workload, maximize market coverage, and drive efficiency (e.g., vertical, region, size). Good territory design does three things:

- Eliminates internal competition (by reducing account overlap).
- Aligns with strategic segments (so Reps can specialize and build credibility).
- Matches Rep workload to account complexity (to load balance).

As territories are assigned, quotas are set as Rep targets. The best quotas are data-backed, motivational, and coupled with a pipeline number.

How the *Push* Approach is Different

Most SaaS businesses set territories and quotas. What makes *The Push Framework* different is when it is done in the order of operations to tighten their linkage to strategy. Under *Push*, you don't build territories in isolation. You wait until:

- The company has agreed on the most valuable market segments (see Chapter 4)
- You've translated the bookings plan into pipeline and opportunity goals (see Chapter 12)

With those decisions in place, your sales leader's job becomes one of execution versus guesswork. When territories are built from your ICP segments and contribution math, they deploy every Rep where pipeline can and must be created.

By the end of these 14 days, you can expect your sales leader to:

- **Define Territories:** Based on your ICP work in Chapter 4, accounts have been segmented, enriched, tagged, and assigned. Total revenue potential is known for each territory.
- **Set Quotas:** Quotas are realistic and aligned to segment potential and historical performance.
- **Assign Pipeline Targets:** Each rep has a pipeline target tied back to the Contribution Model. This is the leading metric that Sales can track and influence every week, to correct a bookings miss before it occurs.

What the CEO Gets

Importantly, you get Rep-level activity goals that ladder up the bookings plan you made in the Contribution Workshop. By the end of these 14 days, you'll have:

- A quota structure that rolls up to your bookings target
- Territories designed for focus and fairness
- A pipeline buffer tied to activity, not artificial quota padding
- A sales leader equipped to detect risk in real time and take action ear

Pipeline Targets vs. Over-Allocation

Another *Push* differentiator: Instead of applying a fixed over-allocation to Rep quota (e.g., "we need 120% quota coverage to hit plan"), *Push* defines a Rep Pipeline Target based on Contribution math. This:

- Bakes in a buffer for lower win rates or delays without inflating quota
- Provides Sales managers a forward-looking metric to coach against
- Ties execution directly back to the shared model with Marketing

This distinction ensures reps are measured against what they control (pipeline activity and opportunity progression) while holding commercial leadership accountable for the assumptions behind the plan.

If you're not using the Push Contribution Model, then you may need to inflate quota coverage or pad attainment goals with a 10–20% buffer. This is less precise than using a true pipeline-based leading indicator but is commonly adopted.

Now that you understand how to leverage *The Push Framework* to enhance territory design and quota setting, let's walk through the steps that your sales or RevOps leader will take to make it happen.

HOW TO SET QUOTA AND DESIGN TERRITORIES (FOR YOUR TEAM)

Once you've completed the Contribution Model in Chapter 12, your sales leader is ready to answer questions that guide them to set productive territories and equitable quotas.

CEO TL;DR

Implementation Steps

Assign Territories: Group A and B accounts into balanced segments (e.g., SMB, MM, Enterprise)

1. **Set Quotas:** Use ICP segments and Contribution Model assumptions to assign bookings and pipeline targets per Rep.
2. **Communicate and Train:** Roll out quota plans and account assignments with context and enablement.
3. **Establish Governance:** Create a review cadence to manage performance-to-quota, pipeline health, and territory yield.

1. What is the size of our ICP account universe?

↳ *Define account universe.*

To size the available market or "account universe," you'll answer this question in two ways:

1. Define the number of reachable accounts.
2. Calculate total revenue potential those accounts represent.

If you are following the 100-Day Plan schedule, then some of the steps you'll take to answer these two questions were started earlier in Chapter 4. Here, you will pick up where you left off to plan your territories:

1. Use your data enrichment tools to pull a list of the A or B accounts based on your account scoring model (from Chapter 5) and related to your ICP segments.
2. Remove duplicate customers from the list.
3. Tag the accounts with Segment, Vertical, Region, Priority Tier, and/or a placeholder for Sales Territory.
4. Calculate the revenue potential for each ICP segment to understand the theoretical max revenue available based on current performance metrics.

Territory Revenue Potential = # of Target Accounts x Deal Size

Use the same historical average or median deal sizes from your Contribution Model (see Chapter 12) or from your CRM.
If using *The Push Framework*: This equation gives you the theoretical revenue potential per territory. Because *Push* already incorporates win rate in downstream pipeline and opportunity targets, there's no need to discount for win rate here. This aligns each territory to its revenue possibility, not its probabilistic outcome.
If not using *The Push Framework*: You'll need to factor in win rate at this stage to avoid over-assigning:

Territory Revenue Potential =
# of Target Accounts x Average Deal Size x Win Rate

This will yield a more conservative view of expected yield per territory *if* you haven't modeled Contribution coverage elsewhere. By the end of this step, you should have the start of your Territory Plan (see Figure 39).

Now that you know how many best-fit ICP accounts are available for your Reps to work, it's time to validate that there are enough accounts available to hit your bookings plan.

2. Do we have enough accounts to support the bookings plan?

↳ *Connect pipeline targets to available accounts.*

Before setting quotas or assigning Reps, validate whether the account universe defined in the first step contains enough ICP-fit accounts to support the pipeline and opportunity requirements from your Contribution Model. If you haven't yet modeled Contribution or defined pipeline targets for the ICP segments, see Chapter 12.

To check whether you have enough accounts to support the plan, compare the number of available ICP accounts from Step 1 against the number of opportunities required to hit bookings from your Contribution Model. Aim to have more accounts available for Reps to work than opportunities required. This builds a cushion for your Reps.

At this point, your Territory Plan now includes opportunities and pipeline targets (see Figure 40).

↳ *Do you have enough accounts?*

If there aren't enough accounts, you may need to:

- **Revisit your ICP definitions** to broaden eligibility (without diluting quality).
- **Adjust pipeline coverage assumptions** (but don't drop below 2x).
- **Improve Win Rate or Deal Size** through targeted optimizations.

FIGURE 39: Territory Plan Step 1: Account Universe Defined

From ICP →		Define Account Universe		From Contribution Model	
Tier	**ICP Segment**	**# Target Accounts Available**	**Territory Revenue Potential**	**Average Deal Size**	**Win Rate**
A	SMB	750	$7,500,000	$10,000	40%
A	Mid-Market	200	$7,000,000	$35,000	35%
B	Enterprise	45	$4,050,000	$90,000	30%

FIGURE 40: Territory Plan Step 2: Contribution Targets Applied

From ICP →		Define Account Universe		From Contribution Model →					
Tier	**ICP Segment**	**# Target Accounts Available**	**Territory Revenue Potential**	**Average Deal Size**	**Win Rate**	**Opportunities Needed**	**Pipeline Needed**	**Pipeline Coverage Ratio**	**Bookings Goal**
A	SMB	750	$7,500,000	$10,000	40%	240	$2,400,00	3x	$800,000
A	Mid-Market	200	$7,000,000	$35,000	35%	94	$3,300,000	3x	$1,100,000
B	Enterprise	45	$4,050,000	$90,000	30%	40	$3,600,000	3x	$1,200,000

If you're including all of your ICP A and B accounts and still can't reach minimum pipeline targets at the minimum 2x coverage threshold, then you've probably uncovered a bigger-than-sales gap close. At this point, you'll need to pause and align with your leadership team to close this gap. Options might include:

- Expanding into adjacent ICPs or verticals.
- Improving average deal size (through packaging, pricing, upsell plays).
- Shifting some of your new business bookings goals to expansion or post-sale goals.

Once you have confirmed there are enough accounts available to hit the bookings plan, it's time to divide the accounts up by Rep.

3. Which Reps Should Work Which Accounts?

↳ *Set rep quota and design territories.*

To design quota-aligned territories, you first need to understand how many Reps are needed to hit the pipeline targets, which confirms whether your headcount is sufficient.

1. **Set Rep Quota:** Start by pulling the segment's bookings goal from your Contribution Model. Divide this goal by the number of Reps you plan to assign to the segment to get a quota per Rep. If headcount is fixed, this is your quota.

   If headcount is flexible (meaning you have budget to hire more Reps), start with a quota assumption and calculate how many Reps are needed to hit the segment's target. Then, sanity-check quota against historical Rep attainment:

   - *What percentage of Reps hit quota last year?*
   - *What was the average attainment?*
   - *How long is ramp, and how many Reps are fully ramped now?*
   - *Is your motion highOvelocity (short) or high-touch (long)?*

Calculation:

 # Reps Needed = Segment Bookings Goal ÷ Quota Per Rep

2. **Set Rep Pipeline Targets:** Apply the pipeline coverage ratio from your Contribution Model to each Rep's quota to set a clear target for how much qualified pipeline they need to maintain at any time. This eliminates the need to over-allocate quota and helps the sales leader monitor productivity weekly or monthly. Calculation:

   Rep Pipeline Target = Quota Per Rep x Pipeline Coverage Ratio

   Note: Pipeline can come from a mix of sources: *inbound, outbound, partner, product,* or *events*. In this approach, each Rep is accountable for converting the pipeline needed to stay on plan regardless of source. In this way, Sales shares the pipeline target with the team sourcing the opportunities.

3. **Set Accounts per Rep:** Use the number of ICP accounts in the segment (see Chapter 5, Step 5) and divide by the number of Reps assigned.

   Accounts Per Rep = # of ICP Accounts ÷ # of Assigned Reps

   Use this to pressure-test whether each Rep's territory is realistically sized. Resist the urge to overload Reps with accounts. Success will be based on a Rep's ability to break into these accounts. The more accounts a Rep has, the less time they'll have to personalize outreach.

4. **Design Territories:** With quotas set, pipeline targets in place, and account volume validated, you're ready to assign accounts. Territories should balance:

a. Revenue potential with rep quota.
b. Accounts per territory with rep capacity.
c. Segmentation by vertical, geo, or size with Rep specialization.

Avoid significant overlap between Rep territories unless using a pod or team-selling structure.

By the end of this step, you have designed a Territory Plan (see Figure 41) that ensures:

- Reps have quotas that tie back to your bookings plan.
- Each Rep has a clear pipeline target tied to their quota.
- Territories are balanced and anchored in the ICP work from Chapter 4.

Designing territories and quotas is only half the battle. Now your plan must be understood, accepted, and executed by the Reps. That starts with a clear, structured training session anchored in the strategic logic behind the design.

TRAINING AND ENABLEMENT

To ensure that your carefully planned quotas and territories are understood and embraced, you'll need to train the Reps. Expect your sales leader to roll out territories and quotas with an enablement session where they'll introduce the territories, explain the math behind the quota logic, and reinforce the persona and messaging guides from the Personas and Positioning you created in Chapter 4.

The training session should cover:

- Their assigned territory (named accounts, vertical, region)
- Their quota (why it's fair and how it was calculated)
- Their pipeline target (what they need to generate to stay on plan)
- Their ICP (who they're targeting and why it matters)
- Their messaging (what to say to these accounts and how it differs by persona)

FIGURE 41: Territory Plan Step 3: Rep Allocation and Capacity

From ICP →		Define Account Universe		From Contribution Model →					
Tier	**ICP Segment**	**# Target Accounts Available**	**Territory Revenue Potential**	**Average Deal Size**	**Win Rate**	**Opportunities Needed**	**Pipeline Needed**	**Pipeline Coverage Ratio**	**Bookings Goal**
A	SMB	750	$7,500,000	$10,000	40%	240	$2,400,00	3x	$800,000
A	Mid-Market	200	$7,000,000	$35,000	35%	94	$3,300,000	3x	$1,100,000
B	Enterprise	45	$4,050,000	$90,000	30%	40	$3,600,000	3x	$1,200,000

Set Quotas and Assign Territories				
Reps Assigned	**Quota Per Rep**	**Pipeline Per Rep**	**Accounts Per Rep**	**Rep Names**
5	$160,000	$480,000	150	Name 1, Name 2, Name 3, Name 4, Name 5
4	$275,000	$825,000	50	Name 1, Name 2, Name 3, Name 4
3	$400,000	$1,200,000	15	Name 1, Name 2, Name 3

Don't assume your sales leader will automatically connect all these dots. Ask for a walkthrough of the session in advance and pressure-test how clearly it ties back to the contribution model and ICP Decisions.

SALES GOVERNANCE IS A COMMON RISK

Once quotas and territories are in place, you are no longer deciding what the number is. Now you're ensuring that Sales is being managed against it effectively and course-corrected when reality diverges from plan. You may pause here, wondering why the CEO needs to worry about sales execution. *Isn't that my sales leader's job?* It is, but for companies working toward their first $100M, unstructured or loose sales governance is often the surprise gap that kills the team's ability to make their plan. Knowing what good looks like will help you intervene early enough to stop a bad quarter from becoming a bad year.

A healthy Sales program has 80% of Reps hitting 80% of their quota. To get there, your sales leader must proactively manage both Rep performance and the model assumptions the plan is bvilt on.

At any given time, your sales leaders should be able to answer these three questions:

- *Are Reps pacing to goal?*
- *Are territories yielding expected pipeline?*
- *Are the Contribution Model assumptions holding up (e.g., win rate, deal size, cycle time)?*

Expect your sales leader to establish three sets of meeting cadences to manage the Reps (see Figure 42). Governance is not just about reporting; it's about detecting risk early, reinforcing good behaviors, and intervening when either Rep performance or model assumptions break down.

Your sales leader will need to bring related reporting to effectively guide these conversations. Encourage them to standardize their agendas and dashboards for these meetings; both tools will help them guide the conversation and keep track of the different plot lines week after week.

FIGURE 42: Sales Governance Meeting Structure

Sales Governance Meetings		
Weekly	**Biweekly**	**Monthly**
• **Rep 1:1s** focused on pipeline health, activity levels, and deal progression • **Team Deal Reviews** to spot systemic blockers, coach live opps, share best practices	• **Forecast Calls** that assess pacing, conversion, and push risk • **Marketing Alignment Check-ins** to monitor SLA performance from Chapter 8 (e.g., validate lead quality, handoff timing, conversion rates)	• **Territory Health Reviews** to assess pipeline by Rep, quota pacing, account penetration • **Contribution Model Tracking** with CFO to ensure that contribution targets and assumptions (win rate, deal size, cycle time) are tracking to the model (more on this later in the chapter).

RED FLAGS TO REACT TO QUICKLY

You will know you need to step in when you see one or more of these red flags come up:

- Multiple Reps pacing <50% to quota with no pipeline recovery plan
- No opportunities generated in a Rep's territory despite valid accounts available
- Territories with excessive "stale" accounts (untouched, unworked)
- Mismatches between leads or opportunities in working stage and pipeline created.

If you're seeing fewer than 80% of Reps hitting 80% of their target despite meeting pipeline targets, then it can be a sign that either quotas are unrealistic or pipeline quality is poor. In these cases, the Contribution Model may be right, but execution might be off or vice versa. Consistent oversight helps your sales leader tell the difference early enough to intervene.

While Sales is designing territories and coaching their reps to *convert* pipeline, Marketing is, in parallel, building the campaigns to *source* it. The next step outlines what to look for in an effective campaign plan.

STEP 12: MARKETING CAMPAIGN PLAN

Owner: *Marketing Leader,* **Duration:** *30 Days (Days 70–100)*

While your sales leader is designing territories to convert pipeline, your marketing leader is planning how to generate it. Step 12 gives your marketing leader 30 days to plan a campaign that, at a minimum, both sources demand and equips reps to convert it into pipeline and won deals.

Marketing campaigns won't work until the first three decisions in this book are made in partnership with Sales:

- A shared Ideal Customer Profile to target **(ICP)**
- A systemic way to convert leads to pipeline **(SLA)**
- Aligned lead and pipeline targets with Sales **(Contribution Model)**

The shared targets and coordination that result from making and executing these prior decisions elevates Marketing's ability to generate and be accountable for, not only leads or MQLs, but now also pipeline and bookings.

As with the previous step on territories and quotas, your role in marketing campaign planning is oversight on execution. This section explains what CEOs can look for in a SaaS marketing campaign plan that implies it's healthy and equipped to deliver on its targets.

Long-Term Campaign

For SaaS companies on the path to $100M, campaign planning is about building a predictable flow of opportunities your Reps can close. That requires marketing teams to move beyond ad hoc changeable tactics toward a focused long-term campaign with singular messaging, clear goals, and coordinated programs relative to:

- **Awareness** (brand, thought leadership)
- **Demand Generation** (lead capture)
- **Sales Enablemen**t (convert leads to pipeline)
- **Customer Marketing** (drive adoption, retention, and expansion)
- **Partner Marketing** (amplify reach and source pipeline)

A pipeline-generating campaign is one that connects with Sales in three critical ways:

- **Shared Theme:** Messaging may vary by funnel stage, but it ladders up to a single, differentiated campaign theme that Sales and Marketing both carry into market.
- **Shared ICP Targets:** Campaign targeting includes the same ICP accounts and personas used to define territories.
- **Shared Pipeline Goals:** Campaign efforts are aligned to pipeline targets from the Contribution Model, which Marketing sources and Sales converts. Both teams are working to hit the same number.

Whether your team is just getting started or running a full-funnel annual campaign, the goal remains the same: source opportunities that your reps can convert.

Campaigns vs. Programs vs. Offers

Before you evaluate a plan, it helps to understand how the campaign elements fit together.

- **Campaign Theme:** The unifying story that differentiates you and connects all messaging throughout the funnel.
- **Programs:** Promotions specific to a funnel stage, designed to engage buyers based on where they are in the buying journey.
- **Offers:** Specific assets or calls to action, such as an ebook or demo request, used to capture or convert demand.

See Figure 43 for an example of how these elements relate to each other.

The campaign theme is a critical piece that enables teams to make an impact with messaging throughout the funnel over months or years. The attribution rules you built into your CRM in Chapter 9 will enable your Marketing team to gauge the efficacy of their programs and offers under that theme.

FIGURE 43: Campaign Structure Example

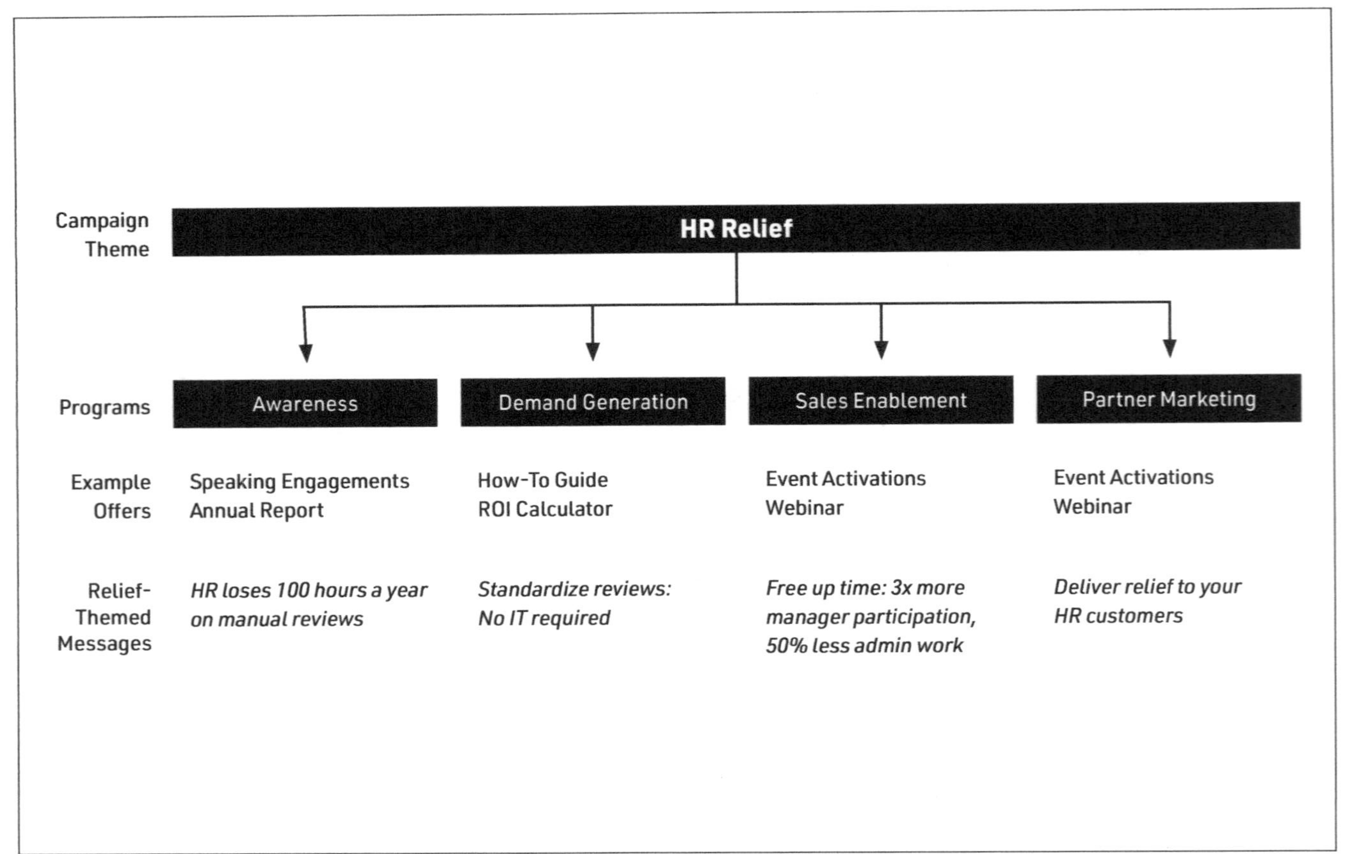

Marketing Maturity: Crawl, Walk, Run

The size and scope of a campaign should match the size and maturity of your Marketing team.

IF YOU HAVE ONE OR TWO MARKETERS

Start with a simpler campaign that only activates demand generation and sales enablement programs. These are the two parts of the funnel most closely tied to pipeline and bookings. This type of campaign would include:

- A steady stream of "always-on" demand generation tactics that are always live in your most productive channels (usually paid search, email, and SEO).
- Scheduled sales enablement plays like webinars or field events support reps in converting leads to pipeline.
- Simple co-marketing packages ("in a box") that are easy for partners to activate and amplify.

These campaigns provide aircover for Sales but may not yet cover the full funnel. You may choose to defer brand awareness, customer marketing, or top-tier content plays until budget and headcount allow. The goal with these types of campaigns is to "turn the lights on" in the parts of the funnel that move the needle the earliest, generating demand and helping Reps convert that demand into deals.

IF YOU HAVE THREE OR MORE MARKETERS

Your team may be ready to run a full-funnel campaign, with coordinated efforts across different parts of the funnel:

- **Brand** (awareness and thought leadership)
- **Demand generation** (offers that capture leads)
- **Sales enablement** (messaging, emails, webinars, and events for Reps to convert pipeline and close deals)

- **Customer marketing** (messaging to support adoption renewals or account expansion)
- **Partner marketing** (joint campaigns and sourcing plays)

Regardless of size, campaigns follow the same implementation steps.

What CEOs Can Listen for in a Campaign Plan

Once your marketing leader presents the campaign plan, your role is to ensure it's anchored to the right theme, aligned to its contribution targets, and structured to generate pipeline for the long term. You don't have to weigh in on creative direction, but you do need to listen for signs that the campaign will support your bookings plan.

CEO TL;DR

Implementation Steps

- **Define Objectives:** Use the Contribution Model to set funnel and pipeline goals.
- **Establish Campaign Theme:** Identify the differentiated point of view to bring to market.
- **Plan Programs:** Build promotions that support demand and Sales enablement *at a minimum.*
- **Set Calendar and Budget:** Calendar the tactics, offers, and content to support the programs; assign owners and allocate resources.
- **Enable Sales:** Package messaging and deliverables for Sales to use.
- **Govern Weekly:** Track campaign production and pacing to pipeline targets with real-time reporting.

GREEN FLAG SIGNS FOR A SAAS MARKETING CAMPAIGN

- **Campaign Duration Matches the Sales Cycle**
  SaaS campaigns need to last long enough to source, influence, and convert pipeline, not just drive short-term activity. Expect a SaaS campaign to run at least twice as long as the sales cycle, usually six to 12 months, with consistent touches across much of the buyer journey.
  ↳ **Listen for:** plans that span quarters, not weeks, and show continuity among stages.

- **Shared Pipeline Targets via the Contribution Model**
  Marketing and Sales work from the same opportunity and pipeline goals defined in the Contribution Model. A strong campaign ties marketing activities to opportunity creation and bookings outcomes.
  ↳ **Listen for:** lead goals ladder up to shared pipeline goals from the Contribution Model.

- **A Campaign Theme Anchors All Messaging**
  Without a differentiated theme, your campaign risks splintering and losing impact. A campaign theme should reflect a unique POV on a market problem and present consistently across the funnel in stage-specific messaging.
  ↳ **Listen for:** consistent theme that connects among awareness, Rep enablement, and customer engagement.

- **Shared ICP and Persona Targets**
  If Sales and Marketing aren't aligned on whom to target, campaign results will stall mid-funnel. Expect your campaign to use the same ICP and persona work from Chapter 4 to inform targeting and creative.
  ↳ **Listen for:** targeting plans that mirror Rep territories, personas, and named accounts.

- **Demand Generation and Sales Enablement Are Both Included**
  Regardless of whether the team is just starting with a simple campaign or is running one that activates the full funnel, campaigns can't stop at the form fill. They must also help Reps

convert those leads into pipeline. A good campaign includes both lead generation and Sales enablement tactics and offers to ensure that sourced leads will convert to pipeline.

↳ **Listen for:** campaign plans that mention demand generation tactics, enablement assets and field support.

Now that Sales and Marketing are aligned on how they'll source and convert the pipeline needed to achieve your bookings target, it's time to set up a system to track progress toward their goals.

STEP 13: CONTRIBUTION MODEL TRACKING

Owner: *CFO*, **Duration:** *5 Days (Days 85–90)*

A Contribution Model is only as good as your ability to track and act on it. This final Contribution step empowers the CFO to govern execution of your bookings plan by leading a monthly tracking meeting that evaluates pacing, identifies gaps, and keeps everyone accountable to their commitments. This meeting gives commercial leaders a structured forum to react to gaps early, as a team, before they become a bookings miss.

What to Track

The CFO will use the output from the workshop in Chapter 12 as the basis for a monthly review with GTM leaders.

Organize the data by ICP Segment and Contribution Source (inbound, outbound, partners, expansion) and plan to review:

- Lead Volume
- Opportunities Created
- Logos Won
- Pipeline Volume
- Win Rates
- Deal Size
- Lead-to-Opportunity Conversion
- Pipeline Coverage Ratio

Ideally, these metrics are pulled from your CRM and attribution reports (built in Chapter 9). If the CRM data is still maturing, then allow the commercial leaders to collect the data manually until the systems catch up.

Remember: The Model Will Evolve

Your Contribution Model reflects the best version of your growth assumptions at the time it was built, but those assumptions won't always hold. Step 13 isn't just about reporting on performance; it's a forum for your commercial leaders to respond to real-time results as a team.

For example, if a Contribution source continues to underperform even after testing or optimization, then the team will need to decide where to reallocate some of its bookings target. If a mid-funnel conversion rate doesn't meet the Contribution Model expectations, then someone will need to own a plan to improve it.

These decisions are made as a group in the monthly tracking meetings. This is why governance matters. Routine tracking reveals where assumptions break down and gives the team a chance to re-balance ownership and re-allocate effort in real time.

CEO Role

A model without governance is just a forecast. With governance, a model becomes a plan. You don't need to run these reviews, but you do need to make sure they're happening. Your job is to:

- Confirm the CFO is tracking performance to the model with the team every month.
- Ensure the full commercial team is attending (Sales, Marketing, CS, RevOps).
- Make sure results are being used to inform adjustments, not just reported.

With this chapter, your team connected Rep-level quotas to marketing campaigns and established a governance cadence that holds both teams accountable to the same pipeline goals, all in service of your bookings target.

Completing this chapter is another major milestone for the team.

With shared execution underway and structured tracking in place, your next job as CEO is to measure how well the plan is working. Chapter 14 shows you how to evaluate the performance of your Contribution Model and spot risk early to maintain a predictable pipeline engine.

EXECUTIVE SUMMARY 14

HOW CEOS MEASURE THE CONTRIBUTION DECISION

Key Takeaways

- **Watch Pipeline Sources, Not Just Pipeline Volume**
  If one source underperforms, you'll need to shift tactics or re-allocate resources to fill the gap.
- **Mid-Funnel Metrics Tell You Whether the Engine's Working**
  Conversion rates, ASP, and Rep coverage reveal if pipeline is moving and closing as expected.
- **Your CFO Becomes the Guardian of the Plan**
  With monthly reviews and KPI tracking, the CFO leads execution governance so you can focus on strategy.
- **Board Trust Comes from Measurement Fluency**
  When you show up with metrics tied to targets, a path to close gaps, and a team tracking performance together, you demonstrate leadership in the good times and accountability in the tough ones.

Chapter 14 Deliverables

By the end of this chapter, you will have:

- Internal Reporting on Contribution Model Performance
- Board Reporting on Pipeline and Coverage
- Contribution Red Flags Diagnostic

Why Measuring the Contribution Decision Matters

In predictable companies, Contribution planning is a system of accountability that drives pipeline creation, supports accurate forecasting, and gives both CEOs and investors confidence that growth is under control. Done right, this is the lever that companies use to grow as one team with purpose and data. The resulting Contribution Model acts as your company-wide, committed bookings plan, but it only works if it's actively measured and tracked.

This chapter shows you how to use weekly, monthly, and quarterly metrics to monitor performance in real time. It teaches your team to treat contribution as a shared responsibility, rather than a math exercise and it positions your CFO to govern the plan with performance metrics, freeing you up to focus on other company strategies.

14

HOW CEOS MEASURE THE CONTRIBUTION DECISION

ONCE THE Contribution Decision is made and the CFO is installed as the plan's governance owner, your focus as CEO shifts to evaluating whether the model is working.

This chapter helps you monitor progress to bookings and sets you up to course-correct before there is a miss.

INTERNAL REPORTING: IS YOUR CONTRIBUTION MODEL WORKING?

The Contribution Decision operationalizes how Sales, Marketing, and Customer Success will generate and close pipeline to support your bookings targets. Once in motion, your job is to track whether each team is delivering on its part of the model.

Weekly (Execution Check): ***Are We Generating Enough Pipeline?***

- **Lead Volume vs. Target** by ICP Segment and Contribution Source (inbound, outbound, partners, expansion)
- **Opportunities Created vs. Target** by Segment and Source

- **Logos Won vs. Target** by Segment and Source
- **Pipeline Value vs. Target** by Segment and Source
- **Bookings vs. Target** by Segment and Source
- **Rep Pipeline Coverage** (rep-level view of pipeline vs. quota)

Monthly (Performance Check): ***Is Pipeline Converting as Expected?***

- **Win Rate by Source and Segment:** Are deals closing at expected rates?
- **Deal Size by Segment:** Is selling price stable across segments?

These internal metrics reveal whether functional teams are pacing to their contribution targets and where mid-funnel health may be at risk.

BOARD REPORTING: HOW CONTRIBUTION AFFECTS COMMERCIAL OUTCOMES

When the Contribution Model is executed effectively, it creates consistency and predictability throughout pipeline creation. Pipeline is the final leading indicator for hitting your bookings target.

Include pipeline metrics in your board deck every quarter to help highlight the team's progress to bookings (see Figure 44).

RED FLAGS: WHEN TO REVISIT THE CONTRIBUTION MODEL

Most Contribution Models don't fail overnight. Instead, they erode slowly, often due to stalled pipeline creation, unrealistic assumptions, or sources that go unattended for too long. Even with regular tracking, progress can still stall when strategic constraints (like product gaps or pricing pressure) aren't addressed.

A Contribution Model that isn't tracked becomes stale fast. If you're not measuring progress against it monthly, you probably won't see the miss until it shows up in bookings. By then, you're also probably too late for a soft correction and a full re-model becomes necessary.

These are the flags that tell you it's time to step in.

FIGURE 44: Commercial Board Metrics Tied to Contribution

Board Metric	Formula	Most Influenced By
ARR Value	Sum of all contracted recurring revenue × 12 months	ICP
New Business Bookings	Total $ of Closed-Won Deals (New Logos Only)	ICP
Logos Won	# of New Logos in Period	ICP
Close Rate	Closed-Won Deals ÷ SQLs	ICP
Deal Size	(Average) Total Closed-Won Revenue ÷ # of Closed-Won Deals or (Median) Middle Value	ICP
Churn Rate	Lost Customers ÷ Total Customers (Start of Period)	ICP
Sales Cycle (Days)	Avg # of Days from First Contact to Close	SLA
Lead-to-Opp Rate	# of Opportunities Created ÷ # of Leads Accepted (SALs) or # of Leads Qualified (MQLs)	SLA
Pipeline Value ($)	Sum of Open Pipeline	Contribution
Pipeline Coverage Ratio (0.0)	Total Pipeline for the Period ÷ Quota for the Period	Contribution
Opportunities Created	# of SQLs or SAOs Created in Period	Contribution

Metrics Red Flags (seen in combination)

- **Pipeline Coverage below 1x** for multiple months
- **Lead Volume on pace, but Opportunities or Wins lag** target
- **Win Rate declining** despite healthy pipeline
- **Selling Price below expectations** in most deals
- **Ongoing opportunity volume miss** from one or more pipeline sources (e.g., outbound or partner)

Team Execution Flags

- Sales and Marketing chase different pipeline targets.
- Sales governance is light or missing.
- Marketing runs short-term tactics, not long-term campaigns.

- Sales enablement is absent or unplanned.
- The contribution model isn't tracked or used.

When these flags show up, first make sure the model is actually being used. In many cases, the issue isn't the design; it's the breakdown in ownership, tracking, or day-to-day accountability. Reestablish the tracking cadence, reset assumptions based on current realities, and reinforce shared responsibility. If performance continues to lag, then you may need to revisit the model itself.

In the final part of this book, we'll shift from measurement to setting company-wide priorities at scale. The OKR Decision will show you how to turn the strategic levers (from the Contribution Workshop and others) into cross-functional initiatives with clear owners, defined results, and real momentum.

CASE STUDY

"I Don't Know What's Working"

The investors of a $27M HR tech company saw strong potential in the platform and their CEO, and set a first-year revenue growth target of 30%. Although Sales and Marketing teams were pushing hard, growth had stalled at just 17% YoY. Both teams asked for more resources: Sales wanted more reps; Marketing asked for additional budget.

The CEO wasn't convinced. New leads were underperforming, ramp time for new reps had increased, and win rates were trending down. Without a clear way to model return on investment, the CEO didn't know where to invest or why growth had stalled.

WHAT THE CEO HEARD FROM THE TEAM

- "I can hit the number with more Reps."
- "Growth has stalled because of (another team)."
- "We're still 17% YoY growth. That's pretty good."

WHAT THE CEO SAW IN THE DATA

- Pipeline coverage below target
- Low number of MQLs for leads captured
- Declining Win rates in core segments

SOLUTION

Leveraging earlier ICP and SLA Decisions, and with help from the CFO, the CEO facilitated a Contribution Workshop with leaders from Marketing, Sales, and Customer Success to define realistic bottom-up targets to reach the company's bookings number. These targets included lead, opportunity, and logo goals from three sources: inbound, outbound, and expansion.

Through the workshop, the team surfaced several key growth levers:

- **Outbound Focus:** Sales had sufficient headcount to qualify the increased inbound lead volume but identified the opportunity to pilot outbound outreach for net-new demand. In the model, the sales leader set contact-to-opportunity rate goals to gauge performance. This gave the CFO and the team something to measure success against.
- **Customer Success Expansion:** Customer Success identified that adding two more account managers could drive a 20% increase in cross-sell revenue by improving coverage and deepening relationships in top-tier accounts, buying time for sales to improve the win rates.
- **Inbound Efficiency:** Marketing flagged a low lead-to-MQL conversion rate, which isolated lead scoring logic as the bottleneck. The marketing leader committed to refining the lead-scoring model to improve quality before handoff to Sales.

While the initial plan wasn't perfect, it provided shared clarity and alignment with realistic and achievable activity targets. The CFO established a weekly tracking meeting and worked with RevOps to translate these commitments into a weekly performance dashboard that tracked leads, opportunities, and deal flow in all sources (inbound, outbound, and expansion), something the team could react to in real time.

Over the following six months, the team used this visibility to monitor pacing, refine tactics, and close gaps as they appeared. As a result, the company reached its 30% year-over-year growth target by the end of the second half. Regular investor updates, grounded in performance against the model, reinforced the CEO's disciplined, accountable approach to growth, and strengthened board confidence in the company's ability to make plan.

PART IV

THE OKR DECISION

EXECUTIVE SUMMARY 15

THE OBJECTIVES AND KEY RESULTS (OKR) DECISION DEFINED

Key Takeaways

- **OKRs Guide Your Team to a Successful Exit**
  The Push OKR Framework maps Objectives and Key Results back to value creation levers and Exit Targets. This structure plots your company's path to exit one milestone at a time.

- **OKR Planning Starts Day 1**
  Although OKRs come last in the *Push Order of Operations*, the work to build them actually starts on Day 1 of the investment with the intake of the investment thesis, Value Creation Plan, and Exit Targets.

- **OKRs Require Prioritization**
  OKRs are how you focus the company based on your instincts, observations, and the goals set out for you by your investor. Your job is to limit focus on three to five objectives at a time that deserve resources, attention, and sustained follow-through in every function.

- **Push OKRs Take the Guesswork Out of Setting Objectives**
  Unlike other OKR approaches, the Push OKR Framework takes the guesswork out of objective setting by using your investment thesis, Value Creation Plan, and Exit Targets as the starting place. This approach gives you something tangible to work toward and builds in immediate alignment with your board on the company direction.

Why the OKR Decision Matters

Push OKRs are the project management framework you use as CEO to align the company on an intentional path to your next exit or funding event over the hold period. By the time you reach this step in the Push Order of Operations, you've caught up on the investor's expectations for exit targets and value creation, built the muscle for cross-functional collaboration through the ICP and SLA work, and surfaced growth levers with the Contribution Model. All of this was preparing you, and your team, to take on long-term strategic execution together.

15

THE OBJECTIVES AND KEY RESULTS (OKR) DECISION DEFINED

THIS IS the final decision in the Push Order of Operations—the one that brings it all together for you as CEO. You've been building up to this point. Over the past 70 days, you've led and empowered your commercial and finance leaders to take ownership of key parts of the growth plan. This gave you the foundations you needed to surface and set company-wide priorities.

OKR stands for Objectives and Key Results. In *The Push Framework*, the OKR Decision typically take about three days to set and activate (Days 70–72). This decision workshop is led by the CEO, with early input from the investor partners, to ensure strategic alignment from board investors before cascading down to the leadership team to execute.

For CEOs of PE-backed SaaS companies, OKRs are the tool you can use to prioritize efforts throughout your team to achieve big company-wide goals over the long term. They break down long-term objectives into near-term Milestone Activities. Success is measured against Key Results agreed upon by the group.

In Chapter 1, we defined the two foundational inputs you must secure on Day 1 of the investment:

1. **Exit Targets:** what your investor expects you to deliver by exit (e.g., ARR, NRR, GRR, EBITDA margin, Rule of 40).
2. **Value Creation Levers:** how your investor expects you to deliver those targets (e.g., GTM redesign, M&A, platform rebuild).

These expectations were baked into your investor's return model. If you don't tie your strategy to them early, you risk distracting the team with projects and objectives that move the team farther away from meeting your Exit Targets. A detour like this is significant; it can put your role as CEO at risk.

The Push OKR Framework gives you a structured way to translate these inputs into a coordinated plan of action for your team to follow. Each Objective you choose maps to a value creation lever (either directly or by influence). Each Key Result supports one or more Exit Targets (either directly or by influence).

With Push, OKRs are the CEO's blueprint for achieving your Exit Targets. If you are following the 100-Day Plan schedule, you'll put these in place as a final foundational step for the team. If you're in the hold period and have not yet established the company priorities that will lead to a successful exit, then you can follow this same process to establish them anytime.

WHAT YOU'LL HEAR WHEN OKRS ARE MISSING

- "We put this whole deck together, but the board only wanted to talk about financials."
- "There are too many fires for us to work on that right now."
- "The product roadmap slipped again."

For CEOs implementing OKRs for the first time, the structure may feel awkward at first because it forces clear trade-offs and transparent prioritization across the leadership team, but that clarity is the point.

Unlike generic OKR templates, the Push OKR Framework is purpose-built for SaaS CEOs scaling toward $100M with private equity backing. It builds on traditional OKR principles, but simplifies the process by using your investment thesis, Value Creation Plan, and Exit Targets as the starting place for your Objectives. This approach helps take the guesswork out of which long-term objectives have to be achieved and builds in immediate alignment with your board on the company direction.

WHY THE OKR DECISION COMES LAST

By the time you reach this step, you've already taken a series of CEO-level actions that have transformed how your company operates and grows. In the Push Order of Operations, OKRs come after Contribution Modeling because you first needed to gather the inputs, the insights, and the validation required to set the right long-term objectives.

- You've aligned with your board on the **Value Creation Plan** and **Exit Targets** (see Chapter 1).
- You've defined your **Ideal Customer Profile** (see Part I).
- You've taught your teams how to share responsibilities with **SLAs** (see Part II).
- You've used your **100-Day Plan** to surface, test, and validate early growth levers through the **Contribution Model** (see Part III).

By the time you reach this stage, you've positioned the CFO as the proxy owner of the Contribution Model responsible for tracking progress against the bookings plan and holding the functions accountable. That move freed you up to focus here: on setting and executing against your long-term company direction.

The OKR Decision is how you'll bring it all together to answer:

- Which growth levers will we prioritize throughout the organization?
- How will we execute and track them as one team?

KEY CONCEPTS OF THE PUSH OKR STRUCTURE

The Push OKR Framework consists of three levels:

Objectives

Three to five company-wide company priorities that you believe will help make your business attractive at exit to the next investor. For PE-backed CEOs, these support or tie directly back to the value creation levers identified in your investment thesis or may have surfaced as gaps or growth levers coming out of the work you've done the past 70 days of this framework. They should complement or supplement your personal vision for the company.

Objectives typically span a one- to three-year horizon, depending on the company stage:

- **Early-growth companies (<$30M–$40M ARR):** Focus on one-year objectives that shore up the foundations needed to achieve scale profitably.
- **Mid-growth companies ($40M–$75M ARR):** Blend one- to two-year objectives tied to scale.
- **Later-growth companies (>$75M ARR):** Introduce multi-year objectives aligned to longer-term strategic bets and exit planning.

Key Results

One to three measurable indicators per Objective that define what success looks like. Key Results are tracked weekly or bi-weekly in combination with the Milestone Activities to ensure progress is being made against the Objective.

Milestone Activities

Near-term initiatives owned by your team members that move the Objective. These are the major milestones, dependencies, or deliverables required to achieve the related Key Results. They are tracked weekly in the OKR Project Plan.

CEO ROLE

The Push OKR Framework serves as your CEO roadmap for leading your team deliberately to an exit. It helps you align the team around the priorities that matter most, organize the work across functions, and track progress toward your Exit Targets. Your primary responsibilities in this framework are:

- **Remind Everyone of the Mission:** Use OKRs to connect the big picture to the daily work. Teams and boards are busy and get distracted. Revisit the growth story behind the OKRs regularly with your board, your team, and your company to keep everyone aligned to why you *are* or *are not* taking on certain projects.
- **Limit Focus:** Choosing objectives is CEO work; only you are positioned to make this call. It will be tempting to include "all the things" in the OKR exercise, but you cannot pursue every growth lever at once. Limit OKRs to three to five objectives at one time based on what will move the Exit Targets most meaningfully over the next 12–18 months. When you achieve one Objective, you can always slot in a new one.
- **Stay In It:** A strategic roadmap requires vigilant management. Drive a weekly meeting to track progress to the Milestone Activities and Key Results. Step in when blockers emerge and reallocate resources when necessary.

THREE CEO DELIVERABLES

The Push OKR Framework delivers three critical resources to support your role as CEO. Each one serves a distinct purpose: planning, communication, and investor alignment.

- **OKR Project Plan:** a practical project management document mapping your three to five strategic Objectives to Key Results and farther down to near-term Milestone Activities. This plan cascades clearly and logically from high-level objectives down to actionable tasks and becomes your weekly execution tracker.

- **OKR Summary Slide:** a single-slide visual used in board decks, all-hands meetings, and strategy check-ins. It reinforces the high-level narrative behind the objectives: what the company is focused on and how success will be measured. This is not meant to show everything. It is a simple and uncluttered communication tool to remind everyone of the company's top priorities.
- **Exit Readiness Dashboard:** this tracks the key Exit Targets your investor identified at the start of the investment. These will be dictated by your investor, but generally include ARR, Bookings, NRR, GRR, LTV:CAC, EBITDA, and Cash Position. OKRs will make progress on these metrics over time.

COMMON CEO MISTAKE: ASSUMING THE BOARD WANTS TO SEE THE DETAILS

Executive CEOs master clear, succinct communication of their vision and strategic plan, selectively leveraging details to reinforce transparency and accountability without overwhelming their board.

Every board is different. Some will prefer high-level updates through the OKR Summary Slide rather than granular detail. This keeps discussions strategically focused and avoids unnecessary complexity. Others might appreciate deeper dives into the OKR Project Plan, especially if they have a particular interest in a particular area or if the connection between your objectives and the Value Creation Plan is not immediately apparent. If unsure, ask, *Would you prefer to stay at the strategic level or see the detailed activity?*

You will determine your board's preference during the initial OKR presentation.

WHEN TO OUTSOURCE

If you have access to an investment-side Operating Partner, this is the right moment to bring them in. OKRs are a key alignment tool between company execution and investment thesis. Your investors are in the best position to help make sure those connections are clear and credible.

If that resource isn't available, a growth advisor is the next best call. They can help you identify which rocks to lift now to influence the larger path to exit or help you diagnose what's blocking progress toward your Exit Targets. You are building for the long term, so having someone who has seen companies like yours take this growth journey can reduce distractions and help get you to the right decision faster.

A third-party facilitator, whether it's an Operating Partner or a growth advisor, can also help if there's tension among the leadership team or if you need neutral help to build consensus.

HOW TO PICK OBJECTIVES

CEOs often ask, *How do I know which objectives to set?*

The answer for PE-Backed CEOs following *The Push Framework* is to start with your vision for the company and then use your Value Creation Plan; your Exit Targets; and what you've already learned through the ICP, SLA, and Contribution Decisions to shape it. Your Objectives should focus the company on what you want the company to look like in one to five years. If you're still unsure what to prioritize, that's exactly where outside perspective. Either your investment team or an experienced growth advisor who has seen the walk to $100M before can help you cut through the noise.

If you're confident about which objectives to anchor on but don't want to get into the weeds of project management, then delegate. Find someone internally to help coordinate the process and track weekly progress. If that person doesn't exist, your investor may have an Operating Partner or a trusted vendor to recommend.

With the right support and focus in place, the OKR Decision becomes your exercise to transform the company in ways that make it attractive to the next buyer and ready for the next big phase of growth. Now that you understand what the OKR Decision entails, Chapter 16 will show you how to get started.

CASE STUDY

"But We Thought Culture *Was* the Strategy"

The CEO of a $22M vertical SaaS company had just led a major product update. They expected new bookings and customer adoption to climb quickly, but early results were disappointing. New bookings lagged behind target and existing customers showed limited interest in the new release.

The product update had been arduous and splintered team morale. In response, the CEO had focused their efforts on rebuilding team culture and improving employee promoter scores. They believed strongly that reinforcing leadership values was a critical building block to outcomes like more bookings and higher adoption rates, so they were surprised when they entered the next board meeting, and the tone was tense. The board repeatedly interrupted the CEO's presentation, pushing past the culture updates to keep the discussion focused on bookings and product adoption. The constant back and forth meant the CEO was unable to get through their deck in the three-hour session.

The problem wasn't effort—a lot of work had gone into company-wide mission, vision, and values training. It was misalignment with the investor priorities. Without an agreed-upon strategic plan or OKRs in place, the CEO had inadvertently deprioritized the investor's growth thesis. It's not that the board didn't see the value in maintaining a strong culture, but that wasn't what they came to discuss. They expected to hear about the company's progress toward growth and exit outcomes, not spend so much time talking about employee sentiment.

WHAT THE CEO HEARD FROM THE BOARD

- *What's your plan to improve adoption?*

- *What's the bookings forecast for next quarter?*
- *"Can we go back to the financials?*

WHAT THE CEO SAW IN THE DATA

- Decline in Exit Targets like bookings
- No metrics connecting culture improvements to Exit Targets
- No OKRs in place tied to exit-related outcomes

SOLUTION

The CEO stepped back and realized they had no mechanism to connect current internal projects with long-term objectives. In response, they rolled out company-wide OKRs.

First, they reviewed the original value creation levers from the investment thesis and aligned with the board on the first three objectives needing to show progress. Each Objective would be measured by achievement of Key Results such as product adoption targets, new logo bookings, and customer expansion tied to specific features.

The CEO then worked with their leadership team to define the planned activities needed to drive those outcomes: marketing campaigns, CSM-led enablement sessions, and sales incentives. These were entered into an OKR Project Plan and tracked weekly with a red/yellow/green system. An OKR Summary Slide was created and shared with the board and again at the next all-hands session to reinforce the new focus.

By the next board meeting, the CEO could articulate the plan to improve adoption and bookings. As a result, the discussion with the board shifted away from questions about the details of the plan to ways that the investor could support some of the go-forward initiatives.

EXECUTIVE SUMMARY 16

HOW CEOS MAKE THE OKR DECISION

Key Takeaways

- **You Are *Not* Starting from Scratch**
  Objectives are built on your vision, your investor's expectations, and the insights you've gathered from the previous ICP, SLA, and Contribution work.

- **This is a CEO Decision**
  The objectives and trade-offs made in the OKR Workshop are CEO decisions. They give your teams the structure, focus, and clarity to execute on your vision for the company and ultimately hit your Exit Targets.

- **OKRs Answer Three Questions**
  This workshop results in specific, trackable decisions:
  - *What are the top three to five Objectives?*
  - *What Key Results define success?*
  - *What Milestone Activities must happen, by when, and owned by whom?*

- **Board Alignment is Built In**
  Unlike traditional OKRs, the Push OKR Framework is built specifically for PE-backed CEOs. Therefore, socializing your Objectives with the board is a built-in step to ensure the plans that come out of the workshop won't get derailed later.

- **This is Not a To-Do List**
  OKRs are long-term strategic bets, not a backlog of everything you'd like to fix. Assume each Objective requires three to five Milestone Activities to gain traction. Overloading the plan can dilute focus, overwhelm teams, and turn interdependencies into bottlenecks.

Chapter 16 Deliverables

After completing the OKR Workshop, you will have:

- Board-Aligned Long-Term Objectives
- OKR Project Plan

Why Making the OKR Decision Matters

Company OKRs are the kind of prioritization effort that only the CEO can implement. The OKR Workshop and resulting project plan are the tools a CEO can use to walk their teams down the path to the next funding event as a $100M company. By focusing your teams on only a few select objectives to achieve at a time, you mobilize them to make a meaningful impact in shorter increments.

This is not a "starting from scratch" exercise. The objectives you set build directly on your vision for the company; are informed by what you've already learned through the prior ICP, SLA, and Contribution steps; and aim to achieve the Exit Targets from your investment thesis. Leveraging this context takes the guesswork out of identifying the strategic bets worth prioritizing in an entire organization.

Your OKR Project Plan comes out of this final decision-making workshop in the Push Order of Operations. In it, you'll define the three to five long-term objectives for your teams to focus on; assign the Key Results that will define success; and map the Milestone Activities, owners and deadlines needed to complete to achieve them. This clarity drives momentum among your leadership team and enables them to trickle down OKRs with their own teams.

16

HOW CEOS MAKE THE OKR DECISION

DURATION: 2 DAYS FOR DECISION (DAYS 70–71)

THE OKR DECISION is how you'll guide your team to a successful exit. This final decision in *The Push Framework* gives you, as CEO, the tools you need to set, measure, and track progress to your long-term objectives.

Making the OKR Decision will be the final collaborative workshop in the Push Order of Operations. Regardless of whether you choose to leverage a third-party to facilitate or you run the workshop yourself, you need to play a significant role. The decisions made in the OKR Workshop are CEO decisions. The framework gives your teams the structure, focus, and clarity to execute on your vision for the future of the company and ultimately hit your Exit Targets.

This chapter introduces the Push OKR Workshop, a one-day strategy session designed to align your executive team around three to five strategic Objectives: the measurable Key Results that define success of those Objectives, and the cross-functional Milestone Activities that drive progress to those Objectives. Done right, the OKR Workshop focuses and coordinates your team company-wide.

You will lead the team to make and buy in to three strategic decisions in the Push OKR Workshop:

- **Strategic Objectives:** What are the three to five strategic bets we'll resource over the next 12–18 months?
- **Key Results:** How will we measure success of those objectives?
- **Milestone Activities:** What critical work needs to happen and who's accountable for delivering it to achieve those objectives?

This is not a blank-slate exercise. The OKR Decision builds directly on the strategic alignment you've already created through the ICP, SLA, and Contribution exercises. From that work, your team now has the muscle for focused collaboration, transparent execution, and a bias for action. These are clear signs of the organizational maturity that you've already led. Now, you'll leverage these values to prioritize the select few company-wide objectives that will influence the direction of the company.

THE PUSH OKR PROCESS

In *The Push Framework*, there are three steps to the OKR Process: Prep, Workshop, Track (see Figure 45). We'll cover the first two in this chapter and the last step in the next chapter.

FIGURE 45: Push OKR Process

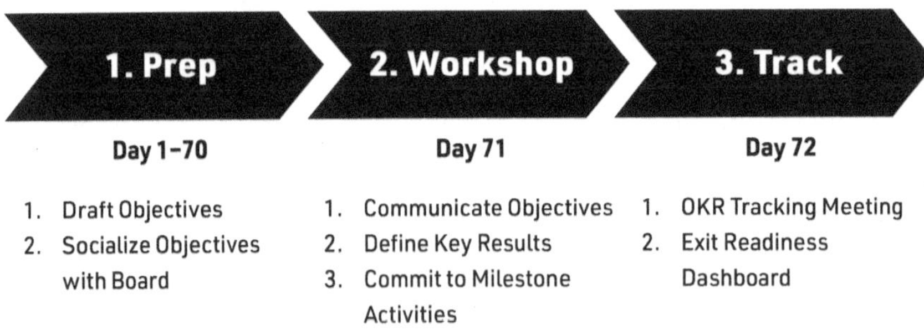

Step 1: Prep

The process begins with the CEO identifying a focused set of strategic objectives (typically three to five). These Objectives are informed by your vision for the company, the expectations and Exit Targets set by your investor, and the growth levers and learnings surfaced during previous three decision phases: ICP, SLA, and Contribution. Objectives should be limited and tailored for achievement over a one- to five-year horizon, depending on the company's growth stage. Before the workshop, the CEO will socialize the objectives with the board to ensure alignment before the team receives further direction.

Step 2: Workshop

Next, the CEO holds the OKR Workshop. Here, the senior leadership team collaborates to define which measurable Key Results to use as indicators of success for each Objective. Once defined, they will cascade down those Key Results into the critical actions necessary for achievement. Those Milestone Activities will be assigned to an owner and given an estimated deadline, thus creating a plan with clearly assigned actions, owners, timing, and goals.

Step 3: Track

Finally, the CEO tracks progress with the team by holding regular check-ins. This approach keeps the CEO in charge of strategic progress, fosters timely collaboration across the team, and ensures real-time action to mitigate gaps or slow-downs.

COMMON CEO MISTAKE: TREATING OKRS AS A TO-DO LIST

It's easy to forget that you are not making a to-do list: You are setting the strategic focus for your entire organization to follow. The OKR process is deceptively simple, which makes it tempting to use it as a catch-all for everything you've been wanting to tackle. Resist that urge. Think of OKRs as a forcing function for strict prioritization. If you overload them, you put execution at risk in two ways.

First, you dilute the impact. Each Objective typically requires three to five Milestone Activities to gain traction. If you define seven or 10 Objectives, you're suddenly asking the organization to execute 25–50 strategic lifts in parallel. Asking teams to take on too much can make them lose focus as interdependencies turn into bottlenecks.

Second, you muddy your strategic narrative. When everything is a priority, then nothing is. Neither your board nor your team will know what really matters or how to move the needle. Without a clear signal from the CEO, teams can default to pet projects or revert back to siloed goals that feel productive but lack impact. You lose the story of where the company is headed, and with it, the force-multiplier effect of coordinated focus.

The OKR Workshop is your opportunity to clarify the top priorities, focus the leadership team, and commit the organization to a coordinated plan that can move the needle.

STEP 14: OKR BOARD ALIGNMENT

Owner: *CEO,* **Duration:** *1 Hour (Day 70)*

The success of the OKR Workshop will depend on how well-prepared you are to lead it. You want to come to that workshop prepared with a set of Objectives grounded in everything you've absorbed since Day 1 of the investment closing. Your Objectives are shaped by your vision for the future of the company and are informed by the inputs you've gathered throughout *The Push Framework:*

- Growth thesis
- Exit Targets
- Value Creation Plan
- Market study
- Segmentation work
- Growth levers identified through the Contribution Model

These inputs help clarify the direction in which your company needs to move throughout the hold period to achieve long-term results. Once you have these, you are ready to prep for the workshop.

OKR Prep: Set, Socialize, and Introduce the Objectives

1. **Identify the Objectives:** This is your three- to five-year vision for the company, grounded in the investment thesis and refined through what you've learned since Day 1. Start with the growth levers outlined in the market study and investment case, and

surfaced in the Contribution Workshop. Pressure-test them against what you now know about your team's capabilities, execution gaps, and bottlenecks. The strongest Objectives influence your Exit Targets, directly or indirectly. If an objective doesn't lift an Exit Targets this year, make sure you can explain how it builds capability or unblocks future growth.

2. **Socialize the Objectives with the Board:** Before the workshop, walk through the draft Objectives with investors. This is about building alignment early, so your team is workshopping Objectives that won't change or be disputed later.
   Questions to ask the board:

   - *Do these reflect the priorities you expected us to focus on?*
   - *Is anything missing based on how you're thinking about exit outcomes?*
   - *Would you prefer to see tracking against Milestone Activities or keep it high-level to the Objectives and Key Results when we present back on this?*

3. **Introduce the Objectives to the Leadership Team:** Once the board agrees, introduce the Objectives to the leadership team as prep for the workshop. This primes the team to show up ready to build the execution plan together in the room. Provide the strategic rationale behind each Objective and tie them back to the Exit Targets. Ask each functional leader to come prepared to the workshop to answer:

   - *What would success look like in your area against this Objective?*
   - *What are the Milestone Activities, possibly already in motion, which align?*
   - *What are the biggest risks or capability gaps in delivering this?*

Once you've defined, socialized, and introduced the Objectives to your team, you're ready to host the workshop.

STEP 15: OKR WORKSHOP

Owner: *CEO,* **Duration:** *4-8 Hours (Day 71)*

The OKR Workshop often introduces change which has the potential to impact every team in the organization in some way. CEOs may find that engaging an external facilitator can help maintain the objectivity needed to guide the team toward consensus. If you are ready to facilitate the session yourself, follow the guide below.

Participants and Roles

- **CEO (Facilitator):** leads the session, presents the objectives, ensures alignment with the Value Creation Plan, and facilitates debate to pressure-test Key Results and milestones.
- **CFO (Tracker Alignment + Pacing):** brings insight into Exit Targets, flags pacing risk or resourcing constraints.
- **Functional Leaders (Sales, Marketing, CS, Product, RevOps, Talent):** align on Key Results, propose Milestone Activities, and commit to tactical execution in their areas.

Decisions to Make

1. **Strategic Objectives:** Introduce the three to five company-wide priorities that will be workshopped.
2. **Key Results:** Establish measurable outcomes that will demonstrate progress toward each Objective.
3. **Milestone Activities:** Determine critical actions, deliverables, or handoffs that are needed to achieve those Key Results.
4. **Ownership and Deadlines:** Define who owns each Milestone and by when it will be delivered.
5. **Alignment with Exit Targets:** Ask about Objectives and Key Results map to Exit Targets or enable future movement on them.
6. **Communication Strategy:** Decide how these OKRs will be communicated to the board and company.

Scan Code for Downloadable Template

FIGURE 46: OKR Workshop Agenda

Duration	Agenda	Owner	Attendees
Prep	Prep the Objectives: Preview Objectives with board and socialize with ELT before session.	CEO	Board, ELT (1:1)
15 min.	**Kickoff & Purpose:** Review Exit Targets, value creation levers, and workshop expectations.	CEO	Leaders of: • Sales • Marketing • Customer Success • Product • RevOps • Finance • Talent
45+ min.	**Present Objectives:** Share 3–5 priorities, invite questions and pushback.		
45+ min.	**Align on Key Results:** Break down each Objective into measurable outcomes that affect or enable Exit Targets.		
45+ min.	**Define Milestones:** Identify critical deliverables, dependencies, handoffs, and risks.		
15 min.	**Resource Planning:** Marketing budget (CPL-based), BDR headcount (inbound/outbound), feasibility review		
15 min.	**Assign Ownership:** Confirm owners and target deadlines for each Milestone.		
30 min.	**Review Full Plan & Pressure-Test:** Run-through plan to validate feasibility, interdependencies, and Exit Metric mapping.		
15 min.	**Wrap-Up & Next Steps:** Tee up a recurring OKR Tracking Meeting cadence. Reinforce how OKRs will tie to ongoing performance management, leadership team reviews, and board updates.		

Workshop Output: The OKR Project Plan

During the workshop, your team will codify the Key Results and Milestones that ladder up to your Objectives as the OKR Project Plan (see Figure 47). This plan becomes the agenda you'll revisit in your weekly or bi-weekly OKR Tracking Meetings to monitor progress and assess whether the work is moving the needle on Key Results.

With your OKRs defined, aligned, and owned, your job now shifts from planning to performance. In the next chapter, you'll learn how to track performance to ensure the work stays focused, Milestones stay on track, and strategy delivers results.

FIGURE 47: OKR Project Plan Example

Objectives	Key Results	Milestones	Owner	Status
Build a Predictable Growth Engine • Support scalable and efficient bookings growth for the long term	• Achieve 90% Forecast Accuracy • Increase Pipeline Coverage to 3x Quota in all segments • Ensure 80% of ramped Reps achieve 80% of quota	Contribution Model across all segments and channels	Finance	Completed
		Deal Review Process Implemented	Sales	In Progress
		100% of Reps Certified on latest cost of inaction	Sales	In Review
Increase Market Share • Stabilize and Improve New Bookings Growth in North America (NAM)	• Deliver $14.4M in NAM pipeline • Close 98 Logos at $49k Deal Size • Achieve $4.8M in Bookings	Segmentation Analysis to Validate the NAM ICP	RevOps	Completed
		Account Scoring in the CRM to Align with ICP	RevOps	Completed
		Campaign Launch to NAM	Marketing	In Progress
		BDR Outbound: territory-based call campaign Launch	BDR Manager	In Progress
		Partner: Co-Marketing Events Live	Sales	In Progress
Turn Customers to Advocates • Create customers who can speak on our behalf	• Maintain NPS above 9 • Achieve $2M in expansion sales • Reduce Churn to <8%	Launch Onboarding Playbook	Customer Success	Completed
		Proactive Health Monitoring Launch	Customer Success	Completed
		Establish Customer Advisory Board	Customer Success	Completed

EXECUTIVE SUMMARY

HOW CEOS EXECUTE THE OKR DECISION

Key Takeaways

- **Remind and Monitor**
  As CEO, your role in execution is twofold: Remind the team (and board) of the long-term objectives and monitor progress toward them. Your job is to ensure your team remains focused on the right priorities even while fire-fighting in the day-to-day.
- **Use the OKR Summary Slide to Remind**
  This visual is your tool to keep the OKR message top of mind throughout the hold. When teams (and boards) see progress toward a clear plan, they are assured by knowing someone is steering the ship.
- **The CEO Needs to Track Progress**
  You don't have to facilitate the tracking meeting, but you do need to attend. Your presence underscores the importance of the plan. In the meeting, your role is to listen for risks, course-correct distraction, and lift roadblocks.
- **Not All Delays Will Be Marked "Red"**
  Some risks won't show up in the status updates as "red." Listen for vague updates, off-OKR work, or silence from activity owners. These are signs that execution may be slipping.

Chapter 17 Deliverables

By the end of this chapter, you will have:

- OKR Summary Slide
- OKR Tracking Meeting Cadence

Why Executing the OKR Decision Matters

You've done the hard work of defining the OKRs and aligning them with the board. Now it's time to build the infrastructure that ensures long-term delivery. Execution is carried out by teams through incremental Milestone Activities, but sustaining focus and driving results over time is the CEO's responsibility.

The CEO has two jobs in OKR execution:

- Monitor progress and remove roadblocks.
- Remind the team and the board of the direction over the long term.

These actions keep the organization focused and on track to make an impact.

17

HOW CEOS EXECUTE THE OKR DECISION

DURATION: 1 DAY FOR EXECUTION (DAY 72)

EXECUTING YOUR OKRS primarily falls on your management team as they work through the Milestone Activities from the OKR Project Plan. Your role as CEO during execution is twofold:

- **Monitor progress** regularly to ensure milestones are completed on time and with the right level of quality.
- **Remind** the team and the board of the objectives and direction throughout the process.

Teams are typically energized when the OKRs are first rolled out. There is likely to be a lot of energy and momentum at rollout, but over time, day-to-day demands creep in, and teams will naturally start to get distracted from these core objectives. Your job is to remind your team and the org-at-large of the mission and keep them focused on the objectives.

STEP 16: OKR TRACKING

Owner: *CEO,* **Duration:** *1 Hour (Day 72)*

You will use the OKR Summary Slide to track progress and regular meetings to update the executive team.

This is a high-level one-page visual summary of your OKR Project Plan. As the work progresses, update it with actual results (see Figure 48). Use it often:

- Present it at every town hall.
- Ask your leadership team to include it in their functional or department meetings.

FIGURE 48: OKR Summary Slide Example

Objectives	Key Results
A Predictable Growth Engine • Support scalable and efficient bookings growth for the long term	Achieve 90% forecast accuracy Increase pipeline coverage to 3x quota in all segments Ensure 80% of ramped reps achieve 80% of quota
Increase Market Share • Stabilize and improve new bookings growth in North America (NAM)	Deliver $14.4M in NAM pipeline Close 98 logos at $49k deal size Achieve $4.8M in bookings
Turn Customers to Advocates • Create customers that can speak on our behalf	Maintain NPS above 9 Achieve $2M in expansion sales Reduce churn to <8%

This visual keeps the company aligned and focused on the objectives. When teams (and boards) see progress toward a clear plan, they are assured by knowing that someone is steering the ship.

Next, you'll formalize a recurring meeting to review progress against the OKR Project Plan. These meetings are critical to keeping your team coordinated and momentum going.

Once you've all aligned on the OKRs, you'll want to schedule a weekly meeting with your executive team to track progress. Use the OKR Project Plan as the agenda and ask each functional owner to update their portion of the plan using a red/yellow/green status:

- **Green:** On track—no discussion required.
- **Yellow:** Slightly off track—may need support, clarification, or reprioritization.
- **Red:** Significantly off track—requires immediate intervention.

These updates should cover both Milestone Activities and progress toward Key Results. Milestones show effort, Key Results show impact. You want to track both.

You can run this meeting yourself or appoint someone to manage it, but either way, you need to attend. Your presence underscores the importance of the plan. If you abandon it, then your team will, too. In this meeting, your role is to listen for risks, course-correct distractions, and lift roadblocks.

CEO Red Flags

Not all delays may be labeled as "red" in the update. Some will be implied. Listen for these risks in your weekly updates.

- **Updates without metrics:** Team members say that "We had good meetings" or "The team's making progress" without specific movement on Key Results.
- **Misalignment with the OKRs:** Teams share updates on projects that aren't in the plan.
- **Repeated yellow:** If a milestone stays yellow for multiple weeks, it could be red in disguise.

Once you've got the mechanism to track progress in place, you'll need to measure outcomes. In Chapter 18, you'll learn how to evaluate performance based on Key Results and build an Exit Readiness Dashboard that ties execution progress back to improved enterprise value.

EXECUTIVE SUMMARY 18

HOW CEOS MEASURE THE OKR DECISION

Key Takeaways

- **Pivotal Step in Your Company's Transformation**
  Reaching this stage of *The Push Framework* marks a turning point in how your company operates. Until now, your reporting and accountability centered on commercial execution. With OKRs in place, you now shift focus from scaling topline growth to scaling enterprise value.
- **OKRs Require Two Levels of Tracking**
  OKR Tracking is your weekly meeting to monitor progress on Key Results and Milestone Activities. The Exit Readiness Dashboard introduced in this chapter measures the cumulative impact of all four growth decisions (ICP, SLA, Contribution, and OKRs) on the Exit Targets and tracks progress to, and readiness for, your next round of investment.
- **Your Exit Readiness Dashboard is a Compass**
  Creating an Exit Readiness Dashboard positions you to control the narrative in tough quarters. From here on out, you're telling one cohesive growth story to your team and your board about how you are progressing to $100M.
- **Key Results Should Influence Exit Targets**
  Key Results don't guarantee Exit Targets but predict progress

toward them. If your team is hitting Key Results but Exit Metrics are flat or declining, it's time to revisit your OKRs.

- **The Board Focuses on Outcomes, Not Activities**
  If the board starts questioning priorities or focusing the conversation on activity over outcomes, it can mean they've lost the thread. That's your cue to up-level the conversation and realign the group on the growth story.

Chapter 18 Deliverables

By the end of this chapter, you should have:

- Internal Reporting on OKR Performance
- Board Reporting on Exit Readiness
- OKR Red Flags Diagnostic

Why Measuring the OKR Decision Matters

Reaching this stage of *The Push Framework* is a significant milestone in your team's transformation. Until now, you've focused board reporting on commercial performance: bookings, pipeline, conversion. With OKRs in place, you can now elevate the conversation by connecting day-to-day execution to enterprise value.

In this last step of *Push*, you'll add a new measure to your board meetings with the Exit Readiness Dashboard. Built in partnership with your investment team, it reflects the Exit Targets in your investment thesis. This dashboard puts you in control of the narrative behind the numbers. It's a helpful tool in strong quarters, and an essential one in the tough quarters. This is how you'll come across as a steady hand on the wheel throughout the hold period.

18

HOW CEOS MEASURE THE OKR DECISION

REACHING THIS STAGE of *The Push Framework* marks a pivotal milestone in your company's transformation. Until now, your reporting has focused on commercial metrics: bookings, pipeline, and conversion. With OKRs in place, you can now shift focus from commercial performance to enterprise value.

To do that, you'll manage OKR success on two levels: performance against the Key Results and a new dashboard for you and your board to track success to $100M and exit readiness.

INTERNAL REPORTING: IS YOUR OKR WORKING?

There is no one set of metrics to measure the health of an OKR. Once your team defines the Key Results in the OKR Workshop, they become the metrics the team will review weekly or bi-weekly in the OKR Tracking Meeting.

Weekly (Execution Check): ***Are We Making Progress on the Key Results?***

- **Improvement on Key Results** as appropriate based on metrics
- **Progress on Milestones** tracked as red/yellow/green status

Key Results don't guarantee exit outcomes, but they indicate whether the team's execution is making a big enough impact. If Key Results are achieved but the Exit Targets aren't moving, then it's time to revisit the OKRs to ensure your objectives are focused on the right growth levers.

BOARD REPORTING: EXIT READINESS DASHBOARD

Once all four growth decisions (ICP, SLA, Contribution, OKRs) are in place, you're ready to build your Exit Readiness Dashboard (see Figure 49).

This dashboard ties back to the key Exit Targets laid out for you in the investment thesis. The example metrics shown here are common to SaaS investments—NRR, Rule of 40, and LTV:CAC—but your version needs to be specific to your investment thesis.

Tracking these metrics ensures that you and your board are measuring your path to your next round of investment at the same time with the same numbers.

This dashboard is a powerful CEO tool. It allows you to control the narrative with the board throughout the hold period.

RED FLAGS: WHEN TO REVISIT THE OKRS

Red flags with OKRs can surface from two places: your team and your board. Your job as CEO is to listen for both.

From the team side, you'll track improvement to the Key Results and progress on the Milestone Activities weekly in the OKR Tracking Meeting. Gaps in that progress will be relatively straightforward.

Harder to spot, but just as important, are gaps in alignment with your board. You've already aligned the OKRs with your investors at the start of this process; now you must maintain that alignment in the board meetings that follow. In that discussion, you'll want to listen for the arc the discussion takes. You want a discussion that is focused on outcomes and not activities.

FIGURE 49: Exit Readiness Dashboard

Exit Metric	Description	Formula	Target/Benchmark	Tied to GTM Decisions
ARR	Annual Recurring Revenue–total value of contracted recurring revenue at a point in time	Prior ARR + New Bookings–Churn	Aligned to board plan and growth stage expectations	ICP, SLA, Contribution
New Bookings	Total new and expansion ARR signed in a specific period	New Logo ARR + Expansion ARR	Set by Contribution Model per segment and channel	ICP, SLA, Contribution, OKRs
NRR	Net Revenue Retention–measures expansion, contraction, and churn within the customer base	(Starting ARR + Expansion–Contractions–Churn)/Starting ARR	> 110% for healthy growth-stage SaaS	ICP, SLA, Contribution, OKRs
GRR	Gross Revenue Retention–measures churn only, without expansion	(Starting ARR–Churn)/Starting ARR	> 85% is standard; > 90% is strong	ICP, SLA, Contribution
LTV:CAC	Customer Lifetime Value to Customer Acquisition Cost ratio	(Avg ARR per Customer × Gross Margin × Avg Retention Period in Years)/Avg CAC	3:1 is a typical SaaS benchmark	ICP, SLA, Contribution
Rule of 40	Sum of Revenue Growth % and EBITDA Margin %, used to assess balance of growth and profitability	(Revenue Growth % + EBITDA Margin %)	Target > 40% combined	OKRs
EBITDA Margin	Earnings Before Interest, Taxes, Depreciation, and Amortization (EBITDA) as a % of revenue	Adjusted EBITDA/Revenue	Target varies by growth stage; often positive by late stage	OKRs
Cash Balance	Total cash on hand available for operations and investment	Cash at End of Period	Sufficient runway to hit next milestone (e.g., 12–18 months)	Finance Plan, Board Alignment

If the board is still questioning the activities and focus of the team, it's a red flag that they may no longer be aligned.

Metrics Red Flags

- Flat or declining trends on Key Results
- Milestones consistently yellow or red
- OKR Tracking Meetings skipped or deprioritized
- Key Results appear "on track" but Exit Targets stall or decline

Board Friction Red Flags

- Board questions which objectives are most important
- Board conversation focuses on activities, not outcomes
- OKR section of board meeting takes too long or lacks clarity
- Too many objectives, not enough traction on any

With long-term planning, it's common for teams and boards to question whether the path is still the right one. People forget what was decided and lose track of the narrative. No one (not your board, not even your leadership team) is paying as close attention to these OKRs as you are.

When you suspect people have forgotten the context behind the priorities, you need to remind them. This is where your CEO narrative comes in.

- Use the OKR Summary Slide to remind everyone how you're driving to $100M.
- Use the Exit Readiness Dashboard to prove whether it's working.

These are your storytelling tools. With them, you bring people back to the big picture and reinforce the long-term vision behind your strategy.

This is the $100M story you've been building over the last 100 days. Now you have the language and the numbers to tell it.

CASE STUDY

"It's All Important"

The CEO of a $10M SaaS company was eager to roll out OKRs after reading up on the framework. They believed it would bring alignment, focus, and energy to the company's next phase of growth. But instead of narrowing in on a few critical bets, the CEO set seven company-level objectives for lighting up activity in every department: Product, Customer Success, Sales, Marketing, and Talent.

With limited resources and small teams, each function was suddenly managing multiple key results and milestones. Execution became chaotic. When board prep time arrived, the CEO created a slide for each Objective, walking through activities in detail to demonstrate progress.

The board was overwhelmed. They couldn't follow the narrative. The CEO was focused on effort; the board just wanted to see outcomes. Instead of showcasing clarity, the OKR deck raised new concerns: Did the CEO understand the investment thesis? Were they focused on the metrics that mattered most at exit?

WHAT THE CEO HEARD FROM THE BOARD

- *How do these priorities map to our investment thesis?*
- *Which two or three of these are critical to hitting Exit Targets?*
- *Are we spread too thin to move any of them forward meaningfully?*

WHAT THE CEO SAW IN THE DATA

- Seven OKRs with minimal traction
- Majority of milestones marked yellow or red on progress
- Stalled improvement on Key Results

SOLUTION

The CEO re-read the investment thesis and pulled out both the original value creation levers and Exit Metrics. With guidance from their Operating Partner, they trimmed the list down to three long-term company-wide objectives, each clearly tied to the Exit Targets.

They restructured the OKR Project Plan to reflect these priorities, consolidated milestones, and reassigned owners so each executive had a manageable focus. Then they replaced the 10-slide board update with a single OKR Summary Slide that communicated Objectives, Key Results, and current red/yellow/green status.

At the next board meeting, the conversation shifted from reporting on activities to collaborative problem-solving. The board discussed strategic relationships they could introduce, M&A targets to look into, and shared insights learned from other companies in the portfolio working through similar objectives. The board, leadership team, and CEO walked away feeling like partners, with clarity that the company was moving in the right direction.

19

WHAT YOU'VE BUILT

DAY 101

YOU DID IT! By following the Push Order of Operations, you've prepared your team for the next stage of growth. They are now ready to take on more capital and more headcount to deliver more sticky customers back to you. They couldn't have done this without you.

By Day 101, you have:

- **Anchored your team on the right buyers** with the ICP
- **Built a predictable sales engine** with the SLA
- **Committed to an efficient bookings plan** with your Contribution Model
- **Created a path to a $100M exit** with board-aligned OKRs

It wasn't easy. You had to bring your executive team along with you to make these key decisions and embed them into their daily processes. That only worked because you took the time to understand how these decisions fit together and because you stayed involved long enough to ensure they were implemented properly.

By forcing alignment in these four areas, you've modeled and encouraged a team culture that is aligned, transparent, and collaborative. As a team, you all have turned these strategic decisions into everyday practices that will continue to benefit the team long after the 100-Day Plan is complete.

THE PATH YOU TOOK

Duration: Day 1–100

You started this journey in Chapter 1 by doing something many CEOs skip: stepping back to become clear about what your investor expected would need to be true to secure the next round of investment at exit.

Value Creation

You identified the Exit Targets, value creation levers, and insights from the market research coming out of diligence to set an early direction for your team. That context grounded everything that followed.

ICP Decision

From there, you moved into the first strategic decision: defining your Ideal Customer Profile (ICP). You inspected your current customer base, enriched your CRM data, and segmented your accounts. You ran the math on where you're winning, where you're overextended, and where there's potential. You made real tradeoffs, choosing to deprioritize certain segments to focus your team and roadmap on the ones that convert and expand better.

You codified that ICP into a usable format and pushed it into your systems and processes with account scoring, personas, and messaging. You aligned your team and your board on which buyers will get you to your targets and which buyers won't.

SLA Decision

Then you moved into the SLA Decision and forced alignment on how leads convert to pipeline. You brought Sales and Marketing together to agree on what "qualified" means, how fast follow-up needs to happen, and who owns what. Your teams defined funnel stages, attribution rules, lead-scoring logic, and email process. They embedded those definitions into your CRM and marketing automation systems to improve performance and predictability. This laid the foundation for accurate forecasting.

Contribution Decision

Once you set the foundation of who to target and how to convert pipeline, you moved into the Contribution Model. This is where you led your team to make commitments as a group. You mapped pipeline sources to your bookings plan and pressure-tested whether current performance levels would get you to that number. You modeled coverage, conversion, and capacity. If there was a gap, you surfaced it early, while there was still time to act.

By this point, you had the skeleton of your commercial engine. You had alignment on focus (ICP), rules of engagement (SLA), and performance targets (Contribution Model), and you ensured key processes were coordinated (quotas, territories, and campaign plans). The last step was to connect it all to long-term strategy through OKRs.

The OKR Decision

You supplemented your vision for getting to $100M with the value creation levers from Chapter 1 to define the company's highest Objectives and aligned them with your board. Then you worked with your team to cascade those Objectives into departmental Milestones that could be tracked weekly to ensure progress.

As you turned these four growth decisions into process, you set up internal reports and cadences to maintain oversight of performance with your team (see Figure 50) and created a board report about commercial outcomes that tied back to your decisions (see Figure 51). This positioned you to influence the metrics during times of dips and declines. Finally, you built an Exit Readiness Dashboard to maintain visibility on your path to $100M and to take accountability for the long-term Exit Targets that formed the basis of the investment thesis (see Figure 52).

This is the path you walked. You successfully avoided the common mistakes CEOs tend to make during their walk to $100M. You didn't ignore your investors' intent. You didn't delegate strategic decisions wholly to your teams. You didn't assume execution would handle itself. You kept your hand on the wheel, took the time to understand the mechanics behind progress, and guided your team toward operating as a tightly coordinated unit. In leading through this transformation, you not only aligned your team, but you also prepared yourself to lead a $100M business.

FIGURE 50: Internal Performance Reports by Decision

Decision	Report Name	Key Metrics Tracked	Checks	Chapter
ICP	ICP Weekly (Execution Check)	Logos Won and Opportunities by ICP Tier	Are we sourcing and closing ICP deals?	6
ICP	ICP Monthly (Performance Check)	Median Deal Size and Sales Cycle for A/B Accounts	Are we winning the right size of deal? Are ICP deals moving faster?	6
SLA	SLA Weekly (Execution Check)	Lead-to-Opp Rate; MQL-to-SQL Rate; SQL-to-SQO Rate	Are leads turning into opportunities?	8
SLA	SLA Monthly (Performance Check)	Lead-to-Opp Rate; MQL-to-SQL Rate; SQL-to-SQO Rate	Are we converting efficiently?	8
Contribution	Contribution Weekly (Execution Check)	Leads, Opps, Pipeline vs. Target; Rep Pipeline Coverage	Are we generating enough pipeline?	14
Contribution	Contribution Monthly (Performance Check)	Segment Win Rate by Source; Segment ASP	Is Pipeline converting as expected?	14
OKR	Contribution Weekly (Execution Check)	Improvement on Key Results; Progress on Milestones	Are we making progress on the Key Results?	18

FIGURE 51: Commercial Board Metrics—Complete View

Board Metric	Formula	Most Influenced By
ARR Value	Sum of all contracted recurring revenue × 12 months	ICP
New Business Bookings	Total $ of Closed-Won Deals (New Logos Only)	ICP
Logos Won	# of New Logos in Period	ICP
Close Rate	Closed-Won Deals ÷ SQLs	ICP
Average Selling Price (ASP)	Total Closed-Won Revenue ÷ # of Closed-Won Deals	ICP
Churn Rate	Lost Customers ÷ Total Customers (Start of Period)	ICP
Sales Cycle (Days)	Avg # of Days from First Contact to Close	SLA
Lead-to-Opp Rate	# of Opportunities Created ÷ # of Leads Accepted (SALs) or # of Leads Qualified (MQLs)	SLA
Pipeline Value	Sum of Open Opportunities at SQL Stage or Later	Contribution
Pipeline Coverage	Qualified Pipeline Value ÷ Bookings Target (Same Period)	Contribution
Opportunities Created	# of SQLs Created in Period	Contribution

FIGURE 52: Exit Readiness Dashboard

Exit Metric	Description	Formula	Target/Benchmark	Tied to GTM Decisions
ARR	Annual Recurring Revenue–total value of contracted recurring revenue at a point in time	Prior ARR + New Bookings–Churn	Aligned to board plan and growth stage expectations	ICP, SLA, Contribution
New Bookings	Total new and expansion ARR signed in a specific period	New Logo ARR + Expansion ARR	Set by Contribution Model per segment and channel	ICP, SLA, Contribution, OKRs
NRR	Net Revenue Retention–measures expansion, contraction, and churn within the customer base	(Starting ARR + Expansion–Contractions–Churn)/Starting ARR	> 110% for healthy growth-stage SaaS	ICP, SLA, Contribution, OKRs
GRR	Gross Revenue Retention–measures churn only, without expansion	(Starting ARR–Churn)/Starting ARR	> 85% is standard; > 90% is strong	ICP, SLA, Contribution
LTV:CAC	Customer Lifetime Value to Customer Acquisition Cost ratio	(Avg ARR per Customer × Gross Margin × Avg Retention Period in Years)/Avg CAC	3:1 is a typical SaaS benchmark	ICP, SLA, Contribution
Rule of 40	Sum of Revenue Growth % and EBITDA Margin %, used to assess balance of growth and profitability	(Revenue Growth % + EBITDA Margin %)	Target > 40% combined	OKRs
EBITDA Margin	Earnings Before Interest, Taxes, Depreciation, and Amortization (EBITDA) as a % of revenue	Adjusted EBITDA/ Revenue	Target varies by growth stage; often positive by late stage	OKRs
Cash Balance	Total cash on hand available for operations and investment	Cash at End of Period	Sufficient runway to hit next milestone (e.g., 12–18 months)	Finance Plan, Board Alignment

ABOUT THE AUTHOR

VANESSA GOOLSBY is a growth advisor, speaker, and former SaaS operator who works with private equity firms and portfolio CEOs to translate investment strategy into scalable commercial execution.

Over the past seven years, she has worked with leadership teams at more than 100 SaaS companies, helping them scale revenue under investor expectations by diagnosing execution risk—the operational gaps that prevent companies from achieving their growth targets—and identifying the growth levers that unlock the next stage of scale.

Vanessa is the creator of the $100M Push Framework, a practical sequence of decisions CEOs can use to translate investor expectations into a clear order of operations that align sales, marketing, product, and finance around the critical moments in the commercial process that determine scalable growth.

She has partnered with leadership teams across private equity portfolios including Vista Equity Partners and PSG Equity, helping portfolio companies take ownership of value creation and accelerate revenue growth through stronger commercial execution.

The $100M Push distills the framework she uses with leadership teams into a practical playbook for CEOs building the foundation for scalable growth.

You can find tools, workshops, and videos at **www.vanessagoolsby.com**

GLOSSARY OF TERMS AND METRICS

100-Day Plan: A project management structure used post-investment to prioritize and sequence high-impact initiatives. Often used at the start of the investment to deploy capital efficiently or during a large effort mid-hold to reach outcomes quickly.

Account Scoring: A process for tiering accounts into categories (e.g., A, B, C) based on their likelihood to convert, potential value, and fit with the ICP. Can be automated in the CRM or done manually.

Account Universe: Full list of accounts that match your ICP and exist within your Serviceable Available Market (SAM). Includes all vended (already buying from a competitor) and un-vended (not yet buying from anyone) accounts that your GTM team will target, segment, and prioritize. This is the operational translation of your SAM—the actual, enriched CRM dataset your team can work from.

Accounts per Rep: Measure of how many ICP-fit accounts are assigned to each Rep, used to validate workload balance.

Accounts per Rep Calculation: # of ICP Accounts ÷ # of Assigned Reps

ARR (Annual Recurring Revenue) Calculation: Total recurring revenue from subscriptions or contracts over a 12-month period.

ARR by Tier: Breaks down Annual Recurring Revenue by ICP-aligned customer segments. Used to assess whether growth is concentrated in strategic target segments.

Attribution: Consistent system of tracking where a lead originated, usually defined by "Lead Source" fields in the CRM (e.g., email, event, outbound, partner). Crucial for marketing ROI and pipeline source tracking.

Attribution Rules: Logic used to determine which team or campaign gets credit for influencing or sourcing a lead or deal. Defined during the SLA process to ensure consistent reporting.

Average Selling Price (ASP): Average revenue generated from closed deals, used to track deal size trends.

ASP (Average Selling Price) Calculation: Total revenue from deals ÷ Number of deals closed.

Base Case: Minimum performance scenario modeled by investors to ensure a return.

BDR Headcount Planning: Method to calculate the number of Business Development Reps needed to support lead volumes based on average productivity.

Blended Cost Per Lead (CPL): Average cost to generate a lead in all marketing channels, including paid and organic. This metric includes the halo effect of brand and content that may not be captured in last-click attribution.

Blended CPL Calculation: Total Program Spend (in time period) ÷ Total Leads Generated (same time period).

Board Alignment: Formal checkpoint where CEO presents a growth decision to the board for validation and strategic input. Ensures alignment with the investment thesis before execution.

Bookings: Total value of new and expansion contracts signed in a given period—core operational metric for GTM teams. Bookings precede revenue; revenue is recognized over time.

Bookings Calculation: New Logo ARR + Expansion ARR.

Bookings Target: Annual amount of new and expansion ARR required to support the company's long-term revenue growth (usually tied to investor-defined CAGR).

Buyer Fit Score: Based on firmographic, demographic, or technographic traits (e.g., industry, company size, job title). Indicates how closely a lead matches the ICP.

Buyer Interest Score: Based on behavioral signals (e.g., demo request, webinar attendance) that indicate buying intent or engagement.

CAC (Customer Acquisition Cost): Measures the total cost to acquire a new customer, including all sales and marketing spend, usually both programmatic and headcount.

CAC Calculation: Sales & Marketing Program Spend + Sales & Marketing Headcount Cost ÷ Number of New Customers Acquired.

CAC Payback Period: How long it takes to recoup CAC from gross margin on new customers. Rule of thumb: <12 months is healthy, 12–18 months is acceptable, 18+ months needs attention.

Campaign Offer: Incentive in a Marketing campaign designed to drive the prospect to a specific conversion action (e.g., demo request, content download, event registration). Strong offers balance relevance (fit to ICP pain) and urgency (clear next step).

Campaign Theme: Unifying, differentiated message that anchors all programs and offers throughout the funnel from awareness to conversion, and aligns Marketing and Sales.

Cash Runway: Indicates how long a company can operate at current burn rate without raising additional capital. Companies typically aim to maintain 12–18 months of runway.

Cash Runway Calculation: Cash Balance ÷ Monthly Burn Rate.

CEO Growth Decisions: The four strategic decisions covered in the book: ICP, SLA, Contribution, OKRs.

Churn Rate: Measures the percentage of ARR lost due to customer cancellations over a time period. Healthy churn for SMB ÷ MM SaaS is typically <15% annually.

Churn Rate Calculation: Customers lost during a period ÷ Total customers at the start of the period x 100.

Churn Reasons: Captures reasons customers leave. Frequent mentions of "low perceived value," "poor adoption," or "missing features" may point to ICP misalignment, Product-Market Fit problems, or service and delivery issues.

Close Rate: Percentage of sales opportunities that result in closed deals; 30% or higher is generally healthy for mid-market SaaS.

Close Rate Calculation: Closed deals ÷ Total opportunities x 100.

Closed Lost Reasons: Tracks why deals are lost. Trends in "features missing" or "competitor advantage" categories may indicate misalignment between ICP and product capabilities.

Contribution: Defined portion of pipeline, bookings, or revenue that each go-to-market team (e.g., sales, marketing, customer success) is responsible for delivering, aligned with strategic growth goals.

Contribution Model: GTM model that translates bookings goals into number of leads, opportunities, and pipeline required by source (e.g., inbound, outbound, partners, expansion), factoring in conversion rates such as win rate, ASP, and cycle time.

Contribution Modeling: Process of aligning GTM teams to pipeline and activity targets derived from the bookings plan. Often facilitated in a workshop format to identify strategic levers and surface execution gaps early.

Contribution Tracking Meeting: Monthly review, typically led by the CFO, where Sales, Marketing, and RevOps assess performance-to-plan, react to underperformance, and reallocate targets based on real-time data.

Contribution vs. Attribution: Contribution defines who owns the number (Sales, Marketing, CS) and informs GTM planning. Attribution explains where leads come from (channels or touchpoints) and informs marketing spend decisions. Contribution = ownership | Attribution = source.

Cost per Lead (CPL) : Average cost of generating a single Marketing lead.

CPL Calculation: CPL = Total Marketing Spend ÷ Total Leads Generated

CRM System (Customer Relationship Management System): System of record for customer data. CRM systems like Salesforce store account and contact-level data used in segmentation analysis and track Sales activities, pipeline progression, and bookings. Must be configured to reflect SLA decisions such as lifecycle stages, handoff rules, and attribution.

CRM Hygiene: Quality and completeness of CRM data fields. Poor hygiene undermines segmentation accuracy and forecast reliability. Segmentation can be run with ≥60% field coverage; >75% is ideal.

Customer Acquisition Cost (CAC): Cost of acquiring a new customer, including Marketing and Sales spend.

Customer Acquisition Cost (CAC) Calculation: Total Sales and Marketing expenses ÷ Number of new customers acquired.

Customer Lifetime (Years): Average number of years a customer stays active.

Used in LTV modeling. Generally, SaaS SMB customers = 1–3 years; Mid-Market: 3–5 years; Enterprise: 5+ years.

Data Enrichment: Process of appending missing CRM data using third-party platforms (e.g., ZoomInfo, Bombora) to improve segmentation accuracy. Functioning databases have 60–75% CRM fields complete/not blank, attention needed if less than 60% fields complete.

Deal Size (Average): Sum of all closed-won deal values divided by the total number of deals. It can be misleading when large outliers are present.

Deal Size (Median): Middle value when all closed-won deals are ordered by size, where half are smaller and half are larger. Unlike the average, the median isn't distorted by outlier deals. Rule of Thumb: Use median, not average, for forecasting, territory planning, and quota setting.

Deal Size (Median) Calculation: Used to arrange all closed-won deal values in order and select middle value.

Decision Phase: Phase where the CEO aligns leadership on a growth decision using data.

Demand Model: See Contribution Model

Demographics: Buyer-level attributes such as job title, department, seniority, and role in the purchasing process. Used to define personas, not ICPs.

Discounting: Practice of reducing price from list or target pricing, often used to accelerate deal closure. High levels of discounting can signal pricing pressure, weak value communication, or need to revisit packaging.

Disposition Reason: CRM field used to indicate why a lead was rejected, recycled, or marked closed-lost. Enables clean reporting and process feedback loops.

Enablement Session: Structured training delivered to Sales Reps to roll out quotas and territories, connect strategic decisions to Rep execution, and reinforce personas and messaging.

Enterprise Value (EV): Total value of a business, including equity and debt, minus cash.

Evergreen Campaign: Long-running, low-maintenance Marketing program with durable messaging and repeatable tactics, typically designed to generate demand continuously over time.

Execution Phase: Phase where the team operationalizes the decision.

Execution Risk: Likelihood that the strategy or plan will fail due to breakdowns in execution rather than in strategy itself. Often shows up as missed milestones, uncoordinated GTM teams, or lagging KPIs despite clear objectives.

Expansion Revenue: Bookings from existing customers through cross-sell, upsell, or multi-product adoption. A healthy expansion motion can reduce dependency on net-new acquisition.

Exit Readiness Dashboard: Investor-facing measurement dashboard that tracks long-term Value Creation using metrics like ARR, Bookings, NRR, EBITDA, and LTV:CAC. Validates whether the company is progressing toward Exit Targets.

Exit Strategy: A long-term growth plan that outlines how the company will achieve its objectives and create value for investors, typically culminating in an acquisition or IPO.

Exit Targets: Investor-defined metrics tied to valuation or desired outcomes at the end of the hold period. Examples include ARR, EBITDA, NRR, GRR and Rule of X.

Exit Tracker: See Exit Readiness Dashboard. Typically reviewed monthly or quarterly with the board.

Firmographics: Account-level attributes such as industry, company size, revenue, geography, or vertical. Used to segment and define ICP.

Full-Funnel Campaign: Campaign that supports all parts of the GTM funnel: awareness, demand generation, sales enablement, customer marketing, and partner marketing.

Good/Better/Best Scenario Planning: Forecasting technique that models different levels of performance based on changes in key variables such as conversion rates, CPL, or Rep productivity.

Governance Cadence: Recurring meeting where GTM leaders review funnel performance, address gaps, and update assumptions related to their functions.

Growth Lever: Strategic initiative that can materially change pipeline or bookings performance (e.g., pricing, down-market product, Partner channel) and tracked at the executive level. Surfaced as an output of the Push Contribution Workshop.

GRR (Gross Revenue Retention): Measures how much recurring revenue is retained from existing customers, excluding expansion. A GRR of 90%+ is typical for healthy B2B SaaS companies.

GRR Calculation (Gross Revenue Retention): Starting ARR – Churned ARR) ÷ Starting MRR.

Handoff Rules: Criteria and timing expectations that define when and how a lead moves from Marketing to Sales or between internal teams (e.g., BDR to AE). Clearly defined during the SLA process to reduce friction and improve accountability.

Hold Period: Typical 3–5 year period when a PE firm holds ownership before exit.

Hybrid Rep Role: Sales role that combines inbound follow-up and outbound prospecting, typically used to test new markets or optimize Rep coverage. Most often used for BDR-type roles.

ICP Tiering: Practice of segmenting accounts into prioritized tiers (A, B, C, D) based on deal value, sales efficiency, and retention. Rule of Thumb: Tier A accounts typically yield the highest LTV, shortest sales cycles, and highest win rates.

ICP Tiers: Prioritization framework that groups accounts based on their fit to the ICP (e.g., Tier 1 = high fit, Tier 3 = low fit). Used to focus Sales, Marketing, and product efforts.

Ideal Customer Profile (ICP): Defines the account-level traits (firmographics and technographics) of best-fit customers—those most likely to adopt, expand, and remain loyal. Used to focus GTM efforts and align the business with the investment thesis.

Inbound: Pipeline generated from prospects who initiate engagement with your brand, typically driven by

Marketing. Examples include website conversions, content downloads, webinar signups, organic search, paid ads, and inbound Partner referrals.

Inbound BDR Headcount Calculation: Total Inbound Leads ÷ Leads Qualified per BDR per Month.

Investment Committee (IC): Group within a PE firm that approves investments and monitors performance.

Investment Thesis: Set of assumptions and growth strategies that define the rationale behind a private equity or venture capital investment, including market opportunity, competitive advantage, and scalability.

IRR (Internal Rate of Return): Estimated rate of return on the investment, used to evaluate the profitability of a PE investment.

Key Results: Specific, measurable outcomes that define success of at least one Objective in the OKRs. Each Objective typically has 1–3 Key Results. Key Results are often leading indicators to Exit Metrics.

Lead Lifecycle Stages: Standardized stages a lead passes through from capture to close, typically including MQL (Marketing Qualified Lead), SAL (Sales Accepted Lead), and SQL (Sales Qualified Lead). These must be clearly defined in the SLA.

Lead-to-Opportunity Rate: Percentage of marketing-qualified leads (MQLs) that are successfully converted into sales opportunities. SaaS companies often see 10–25%.

Lead-to-Opportunity Rate Calculation: Opportunities ÷ MQLs x 100.

Lead-to-SQL Rate: Measures how many MQLs progress to SQLs. Useful for validating MQL quality and SDR follow-up execution. SaaS companies often see 40–60%.

Lead-to-SQL Rate Calculation: SQLs ÷ MQLs x 100.

Lead Qualification: Process of assessing the sales-readiness of a lead—whether an inbound or outbound lead meets predefined criteria (fit, intent, and readiness) before advancing it through the funnel. Governed by SLA definitions to ensure consistent handoffs between Marketing and Sales. Most SaaS companies need to define minimum qualification criteria twice: once before booking a meeting (Marketing Qualified Lead to SQL) and again before opening pipeline (SQL to SAO/SQO).

Lead Qualification Stages: Defined funnel stages a prospect moves through before becoming pipeline: typically: Lead ⇢ MQL ⇢ SQL ⇢ SAO ⇢ SQO. Each stage includes an owner, required actions, exit criteria, and handoff logic.

Lead Scoring: Logic-based method (manual or AI-enhanced) of assigning points to leads based on fit and behavior to determine their readiness for follow-up. Inputs include demographic data (fit), firmographic traits, behavioral signals (intent, engagement).

Lead Score Threshold: Points accrued by leads based on lead-scoring logic and converted to MQL through a score threshold (e.g., 100 points). Thresholds should be tested and adjusted quarterly.

Lead Scoring Threshold Calculation: Sum of (Buyer Fit Score + Buyer Intent Score)

Lead Source: Required CRM field indicating the origin of a lead (e.g., Website, Event, Partner). Used for attribution reporting and campaign performance.

Lead Source Naming Convention: Standardized list of lead source options in the CRM, aligned to Contribution channels (inbound, outbound, partner) and used in reporting and attribution.

Lead Status: CRM field used to indicate the current state of a lead (e.g., Working, Disqualified, Recycled). Required to enforce consistent Rep actions and SLA adherence.

Logo Target: Number of unique customer wins required to hit a bookings target.

Logo Target Calculation: Bookings Target ÷ Average or Median Deal Size.

Lead Volume: Total number of qualified leads entering the funnel (before converting to MQL) within a defined time period, typically segmented by source (e.g., inbound, outbound, partners, CS).

Logos Won by ICP Tier: Tracks closed-won opportunities by ICP tier to confirm execution is aligned to strategic focus. The majority of wins should fall within Tier 1 and Tier 2 accounts.

LTV (Customer Lifetime Value): Total revenue a customer is expected to generate during their lifetime.

LTV (Customer Lifetime Value) Calculation: Average or Median ARR per customer x Average customer lifespan (in years).

LTV:CAC Ratio: Ratio of customer lifetime value (LTV) to customer acquisition cost (CAC), indicating the profitability of acquiring and retaining customers. 3:1 is considered healthy, over 5:1 signals under-investment in growth.

LTV:CAC Ratio Calculation: LTV ÷ CAC.

MAP (Marketing Automation Platform): Platform used to manage Marketing activities such as email campaigns, lead scoring, and lifecycle stage progression. Works in tandem with CRM systems to execute lead qualification and SLA decisions.

Marketing ROI: Measures the return on Marketing investment, typically focused on Marketing-attributed revenue relative to Marketing spend. Whether it includes headcount depends on how it's reported. Gross Marketing ROI includes only program spend (e.g., ads, events, tools); Net Marketing ROI includes headcount and overhead. Sometimes referred to as Return on Marketing Investment (ROMI).

Marketing ROI Calculation: Marketing-Attributed Revenue – Marketing Spend ÷ Marketing Spend.

Marketing-Sourced Pipeline: Pipeline generated through Marketing campaigns and inbound channels, governed by the SLA to ensure timely follow-up and measurable attribution. Companies with strong SLAs often see improvement in win rates for Marketing-sourced leads.

Measurement Phase: Phase where performance is tracked and reported to investors.

Milestone Activities: Cross-functional deliverables or actions required to achieve Key Results. Each Objective typically requires 3–5 Milestones to gain traction.

Minimum Qualification Criteria: Essential attributes and signals a lead must meet to be considered "Sales-ready." Often defined separately for booking a meeting and opening pipeline.

MQL (Marketing Qualified Lead): Lead that meets fit and/or intent criteria defined by the Marketing team, often based on lead scoring. MQLs are passed to Sales or BDRs for qualification.

MQL-to-SQL Conversion Rate: Percentage of Marketing-qualified leads (MQLs) converted into sales-qualified leads (SQLs).

MQL-to-SQL Conversion Rate: Calculation: (SQLs ÷ MQLs) x 100.

Multi-Touch Attribution (MTA): Method of assigning credit for a lead or deal from multiple touchpoints (e.g., ads, emails, webinars). Often used to inform budget decisions but does not imply responsibility for pipeline delivery.

Net Promoter Score (NPS): Measure of customer loyalty and satisfaction based on how likely customers are to recommend the company's product or service.

Net Promoter Score (NPS): Based on customer surveys measuring the likelihood of recommending the company's product or service.

NRR (Net Revenue Retention): Measures the total change in recurring revenue from existing customers, including upsells, cross-sells, and downgrades. Top-tier SaaS companies often have NRR > 110%–120%.

NRR Calculation (Net Revenue Retention): Starting ARR – Churned ARR + Expansion ARR) ÷ Starting ARR.

Objectives: In *The Push Framework*, 3–5 high-priority, company-wide goals tied to the Value Creation Plan and Exit Targets. Objectives are concise, directional, and rooted in the investment thesis.

OKRs (Objectives and Key Results): Strategic planning framework that aligns company-wide goals (Objectives) with measurable outcomes (Key Results) and execution steps (Milestone Activities). Used to translate strategy into action among teams.

OKR Communication Slide: High-level visual summary of the company's Objectives and Key Results, used to communicate and reinforce strategic priorities to the board and across the organization.

OKR Project Plan: Artifact from the OKR Workshop that documents the agreed-upon Objectives, Key Results, and Milestone Activities, with owners and deadlines. Used as the source of truth for ongoing execution tracking during OKR Tracking Meetings.

OKR Tracking Meeting: Weekly or biweekly review of progress against Key Results and Milestone Activities. Helps the CEO and ELT course-correct and maintain execution discipline.

Opportunity: Qualified sales engagement with a defined business need, decision-maker involvement, and expected close date that enters the forecast pipeline. Opportunities typically begin at the Sales Accepted Opportunity (SAO) or Sales Qualified Opportunity (SQO) stage depending on the SLA definition. SaaS companies tend to convert >55% of Sales Qualified Leads (SQLs) into Opportunities.

Opportunity Conversion Calculation: SQOs ÷ SQLs × 100.

Opportunities by ICP Tier: Monitors pipeline creation aligned to ICP tiers to confirm the team is working the right accounts. Aim for 70–80% of new opps from Tier 1 and 2 segments.

Outbound: Pipeline generated from your team proactively reaching out to prospects. Examples include SDR cold outreach, AE prospecting, outbound email cadences, LinkedIn messaging, and direct dials.

Outbound BDR Headcount Calculation: Total Connects Required ÷ Connects per BDR per Month.

Partner: Pipeline generated through co-selling motions or referrals from third-party relationships. Examples include value-added resellers (VARs), referral partners, system integrators (SIs), alliances, marketplaces, and channel partners.

Personas: Fictional profiles which describe the individual buyer-level traits (demographics) such as job title, seniority, goals, and objections within an ICP account. Personas are mapped after the ICP is defined.

Pipeline: Total dollar value of all open Sales opportunities in the CRM, segmented by stage and probability of closing. Used to forecast future bookings and measure sales efficiency.

Pipeline Coverage: Ratio of open pipeline to bookings target for a given period. Used to assess whether there is enough deal volume to hit revenue goals. Companies generally need to aim for ≥3x coverage to hit bookings targets.

Pipeline Coverage Calculation: Open Pipeline ÷ Bookings Target

Pipeline Coverage Ratio: Ratio of the total pipeline value to the sales quota, used to assess the sufficiency of pipeline volume to meet revenue targets.

Pipeline Coverage Ratio Calculation: Total pipeline value ÷ Sales quota.

Pipeline Target: Volume of qualified pipeline a Rep must maintain to stay on track for quota, derived from their bookings target and the required pipeline coverage ratio.

Pipeline Target Calculation: Quota per Rep × Pipeline Coverage Ratio.

Pipeline-to-Win Rate: Percentage of pipeline opportunities converted into closed deals.

Pipeline-to-Win Rate Calculation: Closed deals ÷ Total pipeline opportunities x 100.

PLG (Product-Led Growth): Go-to-market motion with little or no Sales involvement, where Marketing drives acquisition and product drives activation and expansion, often through free trials or freemium tiers. Success depends on seamless product onboarding, in-app conversion paths, and usage-based upsell triggers.

Positioning: Messaging framework that communicates a product's unique value to specific customer personas, differentiating it from competitors.

Program (related to campaigns): Coordinated set of Marketing activities (emails, ads, events, social, etc.) grouped by funnel stage (reputation, demand, sales enablement, customer marketing or partner), sharing a campaign theme and offers. Programs enable Marketing teams to target messages and activities to buyers in specific parts of the buyer's journey at scale for impact.

Push Framework: Book's core execution framework for GTM scaling (from ICP to SLA to Contribution to OKRs).

Push OKR Framework: Simplified OKR methodology tailored to PE-backed SaaS CEOs scaling to $100M. It directly connects company-wide execution to investor-defined value creation levers and Exit Targets.

Push Order of Operations: Sequenced set of go-to-market execution activities operationalizing the four growth decisions (ICP, SLA, Contribution Model, and OKRs), designed to scale bookings efficiently and align the business to investor priorities.

Quota: Bookings target assigned to an individual rep, typically calculated by dividing the segment bookings goal by the number of reps assigned to that segment.

Quota Calculation: Segment Bookings Goal ÷ # of Assigned Reps x 100.

Quota Attainment: Percentage of Sales Reps who hit or exceed their quota. Often used to assess Sales team performance and territory alignment. Rule of Thumb: Healthy teams often see 70%+ of Reps hitting quota or 80% of Reps hitting 80% of quota.

Quota Attainment Calculation: Achieved revenue ÷ Assigned quota x 100.

Record Types: CRM object types (e.g., Lead, Contact, Opportunity) used to represent and track leads and opportunities. SLA stages should be mapped to appropriate record types to ensure accurate reporting.

Recycled Lead: Lead that fails to progress to the next stage in the defined SLA window and is sent back to Marketing for further nurturing. Time-in-stage rules typically define when recycling should occur (e.g., 7–14 days with no activity).

Rejection or Recycle Rate: Percentage of leads disqualified or returned to nurture before becoming opportunities. Spikes in rejection can signal poor fit leads or weak qualification practices.

Rejection or Recycle Rate Calculation: Rejected or Recycled Leads ÷ Qualified Leads (SALs or MQLs) × 100.

Revenue Operations (RevOps) Playbook: Cross-functional documentation artifact that codifies the company's lead management system, including stage definitions, SLA rules, scoring logic, attribution, and ownership. Acts as a build guide for systems and training guide for teams.

Rule of X/Rule of 40: Benchmark that adds revenue growth rate and profit margin; ≥40% is considered healthy.

SAL (Sales Accepted Lead): Lead that has been reviewed and accepted by Sales as meeting SLA-defined qualification criteria. Introducing an SAL stage can increase win rates on inbound leads.

Sales Cycle (Days): Average time to close a deal from initial lead stage to final sale.

Sales Cycle (Days) Calculation: Close Date–Create Date averaged across Closed-Won deals.

Scenario Planning: Collaborative exercise to model different paths to a bookings goal by adjusting levers such as lead volume, conversion rates, pricing, and new market entry.

Sales Governance: Structured cadence of meetings, dashboards, and performance reviews used to manage Rep productivity, forecast accuracy, and alignment with the Contribution Model.

Segment: Group of accounts that share a specific combination of traits.

Segmentation Analysis: Process of analyzing CRM data to identify patterns in customer behavior, usage, churn, and conversion based on firmographic and technographic traits. Used to validate or redefine the ICP. Inputs include median deal size, sales cycle length, churn rate, win rate, and customer lifetime.

Self-Serve: Pipeline generated by users who onboard and convert independently, without Sales intervention. Examples include freemium sign-ups, product-led growth (PLG) motions, and trial-to-paid conversions.

SAM (Serviceable Available Market): Subset of the Total Addressable Market (TAM) that matches your Ideal Customer Profile (ICP) and can be reached with your current products, pricing, and distribution. The SAM includes both vended and un-vended accounts that fit your target definition but may or may not currently buy from competitors. Represents the "reachable" account universe of ICP-fit accounts that your Sales and Marketing programs can realistically target.

SAM Calculation: TAM × Percentage of Market that Fits ICP and Is Reachable.

SOM (Serviceable Obtainable Market): Subset of the SAM that your company can realistically win in a defined time horizon (typically 12–24 months), factoring in current capacity, conversion rates, and competitive displacement rates. SOM typically focuses on un-vended or in-play accounts that are open to switching or buying net-new solutions.

SOM Calculation: SAM × Expected Win Rate on Un-vended or In-Play Accounts.

SLA (Sales and Marketing Service Level Agreement): Shared agreement between Sales and Marketing (and sometimes RevOps and BDRs) that defines how leads are managed, qualified, and followed up. It governs the handoff, timing, qualification criteria, and tracking of leads through the funnel to enable pipeline accountability and forecast accuracy.

SLA Governance Report: Dashboard used by Sales Managers to track lead aging, SLA timing breaches, and stage conversion rates. Enables weekly coaching and performance management.

Sourced Bookings: Revenue attributed to a specific lead source (e.g., inbound, outbound, partnerships). The SLA ensures systems are in place to accurately assign and track sourced bookings.

Sourced Bookings Calculation: Logo Target × Average (or Median) Deal Size.

Source of Truth Reporting: Single, centralized system (usually the CRM) used to track, report, and align on performance metrics across GTM teams.

SQL (Sales Qualified Lead): Lead that has been further qualified by the BDR or AE as having met the agreed-upon minimum criteria to book a first meeting and exits as first meeting booked.

SQL-to-SQO Rate: Tracks how often a Sales-qualified lead becomes a Sales-qualified opportunity. Indicates the strength of SDR qualification and handoff to AEs.

SQL-to-SQO Rate Calculation: SQOs ÷ SQLs × 100.

SQO (Sales Qualified Opportunity): Prospect that has passed the first Sales meeting and met the minimum criteria required to open pipeline. Often gated by qualification frameworks such as BANT, MEDDIC, or similar.

Trait: Single account attribute, such as industry, geography, or employee count.

(TAM) Total Addressable Market: Total revenue opportunity available for a product or service in a defined market if 100% of potential customers are captured. ICP narrows TAM into targetable, high-fit segments.

TAM Penetration: Measures how much of the Total Addressable Market the company has captured.

TAM Penetration Calculation: Revenue from TAM ÷ Total TAM x 100.

Territory Revenue Potential: Total theoretical bookings that can be generated from a defined territory or segment based on ICP-fit accounts and average deal size.

Territory Revenue Potential Calculation: # of Target Accounts × Avg Deal Size (if not using Contribution Modeling, win rate should also be factored in).

Time to First Contact: Elapsed time between a lead entering a stage (e.g., SQL) and the first outreach attempt by a Rep. Rule of thumb: Reps attempt to contact new inbound or routed leads within 24 hours or as defined in the SLA.

Territory Planning: Process of dividing sales markets into defined segments (e.g., by geography, industry, or account size) and assigning them to sales reps or teams to ensure fair distribution of opportunities and market coverage.

Technographics: Technology-related attributes at the account level, such as which software platforms, infrastructure, or tools are in use. These often indicate likelihood of product fit or adoption.

Time in Stage: Duration a lead remains in a specific funnel stage before progressing, recycling, or being closed. For example, BDRs are often expected to work a lead within 10–15 business days before recycling or escalating.

UTM Parameters (Urchin Tracking Module): Tags appended to URLs to track the performance of Marketing campaigns. Used by MAPs and CRMs to auto-populate attribution fields. Example parameters are utm_source, utm_medium, utm_campaign.

Value Creation: Process of increasing a company's enterprise value through levers related to profitable growth, operational efficiency, and multiple expansion. In a PE context, Value Creation is driven by a repeatable operating rhythm that compounds ARR growth and margin improvement over time.

Value Creation Levers: Hypothesized strategies (e.g., M&A, upmarket expansion) believed to drive growth and value.

Value Creation Plan (VCP): Roadmap of strategic initiatives aimed at increasing enterprise value over the hold period, often developed by or in partnership with investors.

INDEX

D

E

F

G

H

I

K

L

M

O

P

Q

R

S

T

U

V

www.ingramcontent.com/pod-product-compliance
Lightning Source LLC
LaVergne TN
LVHW091122080826
845145LV00008B/2010
* 9 7 8 1 9 6 3 5 4 9 3 0 0 *